W9-BHL-277

BECOMING GOD'S
CHAMPION

KAY ARTHUR
JANNA ARNDT

HARVEST HOUSE PUBLISHERS
EUGENE, OREGON

Scripture quotations in this book are taken from the New American Standard Bible ®, © 1960, 1962, 1963, 1968, 1971, 1972, 1973, 1975, 1977, 1995 by The Lockman Foundation. Used by permission. (www.Lockman.org)

DISCOVER 4 YOURSELF is a registered trademark of The Hawkins Children's LLC. Harvest House Publishers, Inc., is the exclusive licensee of the federally registered trademark DISCOVER 4 YOURSELF.

Illustrations © by Steve Bjorkman

Cover by Left Coast Design, Portland, Oregon

Discover 4 Yourself® Inductive Bible Studies for Kids
BECOMING GOD'S CHAMPION
Copyright © 2009 by Precept Ministries International
Published by Harvest House Publishers
Eugene, Oregon 97402
www.harvesthousepublishers.com

ISBN 978-0-7369-2594-5 (pbk.)
ISBN 978-0-7369-3550-0 (eBook)

All rights reserved. No part of this publication may be reproduced, stored in a retrieval system, or transmitted in any form or by any means—electronic, mechanical, digital, photocopy, recording, or any other—except for brief quotations in printed reviews, without the prior permission of the publisher.

Printed in the United States of America

14 15 16 17 18 19 20   / ML-SK / 10 9 8 7 6 5 4 3

CONTENTS

Becoming God's Champion—
A Bible Study *You* Can Do!

BECOMING GOD'S CHAMPION—
A BIBLE STUDY YOU CAN DO!

Hey guys, guess what? Molly, Sam (the great, face-licking detective beagle), and I are getting ready for a great new Bible adventure. By the way, my name is Max, and we want you to join us as we go to a summer sports camp to train to become champions for God. Doesn't that sound exciting?

While we are at camp competing in our summer games, we are also going to look at our official Rulebook, the Bible, to learn about a letter that one of God's champions wrote to his son in the faith. WHO wrote this awesome letter that shows us how to be a champion for God? WHAT is the good news about Jesus Christ? Have you believed it? WHOM are you going to pass the baton, the good news about Jesus Christ, on to? HOW are you going to stay faithful and run the race when others quit and turn away? And WHY is it so important for you to know God's Word for yourself?

You'll get the answers to all these questions and win the race that God has set for you, as you study the Bible, the source of all truth, and ask God's Spirit to lead and guide you. Psalm 119:102 shows us that God is the one who teaches us. Isn't that cool? God is our Coach!

You also have this book, which is an inductive Bible study. The word *inductive* means you go straight to the Bible *yourself* to investigate what the book of 2 Timothy shows you about guarding the gospel and entrusting it to others. In inductive Bible study, you discover 4 yourself what the Bible says and means.

Aren't you excited? Grab your official Rulebook and get ready for an *awesome* summer as you train to become God's champion by knowing His Word so you can pass the baton to others, finish the course, and receive a crown that will last forever!

THINGS YOU'LL NEED

New American Standard Bible (updated edition)—preferably the *New Inductive Study Bible* (NISB)
Have you gotten yours yet?

Pen or pencil

A dictionary

Colored pencils

This workbook

Index cards

1

GUARD THE TREASURE

2 TIMOTHY 1–4

"Hey guys!" Max called out. "Welcome to summer sports camp! Aren't you excited? You're going to get to compete in the same kind of games that they have in the Olympics. We're going to train to be true champions for God. Why don't you head to your rooms and unpack. Then we'll meet you at Hardaway Hall to begin our training on becoming God's champion."

DAY ONE

EXERCISE YOUR MIND

"Great, you're here!" Molly called out. "Uh-oh, you better watch out. Sam is going to be pretty excited to have you here at our summer sports camp. He has been practicing and practicing his events since Uno the beagle won the best of breed at the Westminster dog show. Sam knows he is an awesome detective beagle, and now he wants to be a champion too! Oh no, it's too late—he sees you, so get ready for a good face licking."

"Wait, Sam!" Max yelled out. "Don't jump up on them!" Oops—too late. Sam sure gets excited when he sees you. Hurry up and give him a treat so he'll get down and quit licking. All right, now that you're here and Sam is munching on his treat, we can get started on our first training exercise.

Molly smiled, "WHAT is the first thing you need to do before you get started? Do you remember? You've got it! P __ __ __!

"Remember, Bible study should always begin with prayer. We need to ask God to help us understand what the Bible says and to direct us by His Holy Spirit so we can make sure we understand His Word and handle it accurately."

Now that we've talked to God, our "heavenly Coach," and asked for His help, we are ready to do our first exercise to train our mind. Did you know that the Bible is made up of different kinds of literature? Some books in the Bible are historical, some are biographical, and others are poetic, proverbial, prophetic, epistles (letters), or a combination—like the book of Daniel, which is both a historical and a prophetic book. We are going to study the book of 2 Timothy, which is an epistle (a letter).

When we study a letter in the Bible, we do it differently than we would study a historical book. The first thing we need to do when we study any letter in the New Testament is to read the whole letter to find out WHO wrote the letter, to WHOM it was written, WHAT the letter is about, and WHY it was written.

When we read a letter today, sometimes we don't know who wrote the letter until we see the signature at the end. But in Bible times the writer of the letter identified himself immediately instead of waiting until the end of the letter. The letter was signed at the beginning!

Our first exercise is to read the letter to find out WHO wrote it and to WHOM it was written. Let's get started by reading 2 Timothy 1 and looking for the people.

Turn to your Observation Worksheets on page 160. Observation Worksheets have the Bible text printed out for you to use as you do your study on 2 Timothy.

Read 2 Timothy 1 and mark every reference to the author of the book (WHO wrote the letter) in a special way. Color him blue.

Mark every reference to the recipient (to WHOM it was written) by coloring him orange.

Mark all of the other names (*not* including God or Jesus) by coloring them pink.

And don't forget to make sure you mark the pronouns that refer to the author, the recipient, and the other people, each in the right color.

What's a pronoun? Check out the Max and Molly's exercise manual below:

Pronouns

Pronouns are words that take the place of nouns. A noun is a person, place, or thing. A pronoun stands in for a noun! Here's an example: "Max is an awesome runner. He can't wait to compete on the relay team." The word *he* is a pronoun because it takes the place of Max's name in the second sentence. *He* is another word we use to refer to Max.

Watch for these other pronouns when you are marking people:

I, me, my, mine   it, its

you, your, yours   we, us, our, ours

he, him, his   she, her, hers

they, them, their, theirs

2 Timothy 1:1 WHO wrote this letter? _____

2 Timothy 1:2 To WHOM was the letter written?

_____

Now that we have discovered that Paul wrote this letter to Timothy, let's find out WHAT we can learn about Paul. Look at every place you marked *Paul* by coloring him blue on your Observation Worksheet in 2 Timothy 1, and fill in the list in the box on the next page.

WHAT I Learned About Paul

2 Timothy 1:1 Paul is an _____ of _____
_____.

2 Timothy 1:3 Paul t __ __ __ __ s God.

2 Timothy 1:3 Paul s __ __ __ __ s God with a _____

_____. Paul p __ __ __ s for Timothy.

2 Timothy 1:4 Paul l __ __ __ s to _____ Timothy so
that he will be filled with _____.

2 Timothy 1:8 Paul is the Lord's p __ __ __ __ __ __ __.
Paul is _____ for the g __ __ __ __ __.

2 Timothy 1:11 Paul was appointed a _____
and an _____ and a _____ for the
gospel.

2 Timothy 1:12 Paul s __ __ __ __ __ s for the gospel.
Paul is not a __ __ __ __ __ __ of the gospel. Paul is
convinced that _____ is able to _____
what he has _____ to Him until that day.

2 Timothy 1:16-17 Paul is r __ __ __ __ __ __ __ __ by
Onesiphorus. Paul is in c __ __ __ __ __ in R __ __ __.

Fantastic! Just look at what you have discovered by looking
at one person in a small section of this letter. You discovered that
Paul was an apostle, of Jesus Christ. That means he was a messen-
ger of the good news about Jesus Christ. He was appointed a

preacher, an apostle and a teacher. Paul is serving God by telling other people the good news about Jesus Christ.

HOW can you serve God? Write out one way that you can serve God. _____

_____

Looking at your list, WHAT do you see about Paul's circumstances in 2 Timothy 1:8,16?

1:8 Paul is _____ for the g __ __ __ __ __.

He is the Lord's p __ __ __ __ __ __ __.

1:16 Paul is in c__ __ __ __ s.

Wow! It looks like Paul is in some pretty hard circumstances. He is in prison, suffering for the gospel. This question you just answered about Paul's circumstances gives us a chance to talk about something important called *context.*

Context is a combination of two words: *con,* which means "with," and *text,* which means "what is written." Context is the setting in which something is found. When you look for context in the Bible, you look at the verses surrounding the passage you are studying. Then you also think about where the passage fits in the big picture of the chapter you are studying, how it fits in the book, and then how it fits into the whole Bible.

Context also includes these:

- The place where something happens. (This is **geographical** context. WHERE is this happening? Is this taking place in Rome, Israel, or the United States?)

- The time in history when an event happens. (This is **historical** context. WHEN is this happening? Is it before Jesus died on the cross or after?)

- The customs of a group of people. (This is **cultural** context. WHAT did people in Bible times wear? Did they wear tunics or shorts and T-shirts?)

It's always important to be on the lookout for the context because it helps you discover WHAT the Bible is saying. WHAT do Paul's circumstances help you see about the time when Paul lived (the historical context)? Just from what you have seen today, do you think it was an easy time in history to be a Christian, or do you think Christians were persecuted and suffering during this time in history? Write out what you think on the line below.

_____

All right! Today we started getting the big picture of Paul's letter to Timothy, and we discovered that Paul is in prison, suffering for the gospel. We'll get the details later.

As we head outside to practice carrying the flags for the opening ceremony of our summer sports camp, look at the flags of the different countries we will represent here at camp.

Each flag has a number inside the ball at the top of the flagpole. Look at the number inside the ball and find the matching blank below. Write the word written on the flagpole on the correct blank to solve this week's verse. Then turn to 2 Timothy 1 and find the reference for this verse.

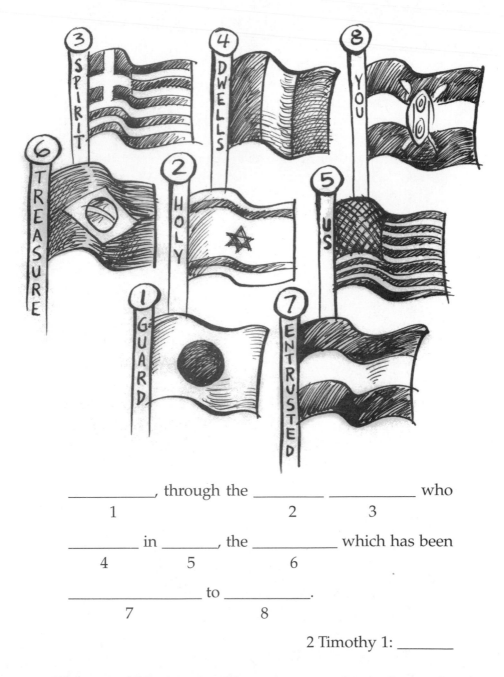

_____, through the _____ _____ who
     1   2   3

_____ in _____, the _____ which has been
    4   5   6

_____ to _____.
     7   8

2 Timothy 1: _____

Way to go! Now write this verse out and practice saying it three times in a row out loud today!

DAY TWO

REFUELING YOUR BODY

Good morning! Did you get a good night's sleep? You know it's very important for athletes to get eight to ten hours of sleep at night so their bodies can rest, recover, and restore their energy. Let's go through the breakfast line and get our food so we can fuel our bodies and get back to our training. Our minds and our muscles need a good breakfast so they will be ready to do some hard work to help us become true Olympians for God!

That was soooo good! We saw you feeding Sam a little bacon under the table. He is going to love you forever! Now that we have rested and refueled, we need to get back to the letter of 2 Timothy. Studying the Bible is the most important exercise we can ever do!

Today we are going to continue to get the big picture of our letter. Turn to page 160 and read 2 Timothy 1 again.

Now, look at every place where you marked *Timothy* in orange yesterday on your Observation Worksheet. In the box on the next page, make a list of what you learned about Timothy.

WHAT I Learned About Timothy

2 Timothy 1:2 Timothy is Paul's _____

_____.

2 Timothy 1:5 Timothy has a _____

_____, which he received from his

_____ L__ __ __ and his _____

E __ __ __ __ __.

2 Timothy 1:6 The g __ __ __ of G __ __ is in Timothy.

2 Timothy 1:14 The _____ has been entrusted to Timothy.

Isn't that awesome? Timothy is Paul's beloved son. That doesn't mean Paul was really Timothy's father; it means Timothy has a close relationship to Paul, like a father-son relationship. Timothy is Paul's son as a believer in Jesus. We see that Timothy has a sincere faith—that's a faith that is real! Timothy learned about faith from his mother and grandmother. And he has been entrusted with the gospel so he can share the good news about Jesus with others!

Look at the other people in 2 Timothy 1 that you colored pink. Let's ask the 5 W's and an H to get some details on these people. WHAT are the 5 W's and an H? They are the WHO, WHAT, WHERE, WHEN, WHY, and HOW questions.

1. Asking WHO helps you find out...

   WHO wrote this?

   WHOM are we reading about?

   WHOM was it written to?

   WHO said this or did that?

2. WHAT helps you understand...

WHAT the author is talking about.

WHAT are the main things that happen?

3. WHERE helps you learn…

   WHERE something happened.

   WHERE did they go?

   WHERE was this said?

   When we discover a "where," we double underline the "where" in green.

4. WHEN tells us about time. We mark it with a green clock 🕐 or a green circle like this: ○ .

   WHEN tells us…

   WHEN did this event happen? Or WHEN will it happen?

   WHEN did the main characters do something? This helps us to follow the order of events.

5. WHY asks questions like…

   WHY did he say that?

   WHY did they go there?

   WHY did this happen?

6. HOW lets you figure out things like…

   HOW something is to be done.

   HOW people knew something had happened.

Now, as you ask the 5 W's and an H about these other people, you are going to see a *contrast*. A contrast shows two things that are different or opposite, like light and dark.

   2 Timothy 1:15 WHO are the people mentioned in this verse?

1. All who are in _____

2. P __ __ __ __ __ __ __

3. H __ __ __ __ __ __ __ __ __

2 Timothy 1:15 WHAT did this group of people in Asia do?

They _____ _____ from Paul.

2 Timothy 1:16-18 WHO is the person mentioned in these verses?

_____

2 Timothy 1:16-18 WHAT did Onesiphorus do?_____

_____

_____

Did you see the contrast, the difference in these people? Those who were unfaithful turned away from Paul, but the one who was faithful was not ashamed of Paul. WHO was faithful? WHO supported Paul? And WHO are the unfaithful, those who turned away?

Faithful: _____

Unfaithful: _____

Now look at 2 Timothy 1:17. WHERE was Onesiphorus

when he found Paul? _____

All right! You just uncovered another clue in our setting. You discovered WHERE Paul is.

WHERE is Paul in prison? _____

Way to go! Tomorrow we will continue to get the big picture of 2 Timothy. Don't forget to practice your memory verse!

DAY THREE

HIT THE TRAINING FIELD

"Hey, Max, that was an awesome long jump!" Molly told Max as they walked off the training field.

"Thanks, Molly. I noticed you cut a few seconds off your time as you were practicing your sprints," Max smiled.

"I can't believe it!" Molly handed Max a towel. "I guess all those exercises Coach Neighbors is making us do are paying off."

"They sure are. Coach Neighbors is not only a great teacher, teaching us the skills we need to improve in each one of our events. He's also a great encourager, just like Paul. We better get

to the showers and clean up so we can read more of Paul's letter to Timothy."

"All right. I'll meet you at Hardaway Hall."

Now that we have practiced for our events, let's get back to 2 Timothy. Training our minds and winning the gold for God takes hard work and self-discipline, just like training our bodies. Don't forget to talk to God and ask for His help.

We are ready to read another section of our letter. Turn to page 161 and read 2 Timothy 2. Mark Paul by coloring him blue, mark Timothy by coloring him orange, and color all the other people pink. Don't mark the soldier, athlete, and farmer pink—they aren't real people in the text; they are just illustrations. Don't forget to mark your pronouns!

Let's make a list on Paul in the box below.

WHAT I Learned About Paul

2 Timothy 2:3 Paul _____ hardship as a

good _____ of _____ _____ .

2 Timothy 2:8-9 Paul _____ hardship even

to _____ as a _____ for the

g — — — — —.

2 Timothy 2:10 Paul _____ all things for the

sake of those who are _____.

Only one thing is mentioned about Timothy in 2 Timothy 2. 2 Timothy 2:1 HOW is Timothy described in this verse?

He is Paul's _____.

The other places where we marked *Timothy* in 2 Timothy 2 contain instructions to Timothy rather than information about Timothy. So let's do some *cross-referencing* to get more information about Timothy. Cross-referencing means looking at other passages of Scripture and comparing Scripture with Scripture.

Pull out your official Rulebook, your Bible. Look up and read Acts 16:1-5. HOW is Timothy described?

Acts 16:1 A _____ , the son of a _____

woman who was a _____, but his father was

a _____.

Acts 16:2 Timothy was _____ _____ of by the

_____.

Acts 16:3 Paul c __ __ __ __ __ __ __ __ __ __ Timothy.

Look up and read 1 Corinthians 4:17. HOW is Timothy described?

_____

_____

Look up and read Philippians 2:19-24.

WHAT do you learn about Timothy?

Philippians 2:20 Timothy is a _____

_____ who will genuinely be _____

for other's_____.

Philippians 2:22 Timothy has proven _____. He

s __ __ __ __ with Paul in the _____

of the _____ like a _____ serving his

_____.

Amazing! Timothy is spoken well of, he has proven worth, and he genuinely cares for the welfare of others. Timothy has been faithful in serving with Paul in furthering the gospel. Are you like Timothy? Do you genuinely care for others? Name one way you care for other people. _____

_____

Now look at where you marked the other names in 2 Timothy 2.

2 Timothy 2:17-18 WHO are the people mentioned?

_____

_____

2 Timothy 2:17-18 WHAT do we learn about these men?

_____

_____

Are they teaching what is true? _____

WHAT are they teaching that is untrue?

_____

_____

Do these men sound like "faithful men," true believers in Jesus?_____

Great work! You got a few more pieces to Paul's letter. Have you noticed a word that is repeated in 2 Timothy 1–2 and that seems to be a very important subject in this letter? Fill in the blanks below if you know what this key word is.

Paul is suffering for the g __ __ __ __ __ .

Now, keep your eyes open—you want to see if this word or

any synonyms for this word show up in the next two chapters of Paul's letter. By the way, one of the words in your memory verse is a synonym for this word. Do you know what the word is? Fill in the blanks if you do.

T _ _ _ _ _ e

Fantastic! Now go out and take a couple of laps around the track as you practice your memory verse!

DAY FOUR

PERSEVERE—DON'T GIVE UP!

"Okay, guys," Coach Neighbors called out. "You've done a great job on your relay drills today. Remember, when you get tired, hang in there—don't give up! Winning the race is about persevering even when you're tired and the going gets tough.

"Let's take a break, eat a snack, and give our bodies a little rest while we work on our letter of 2 Timothy. Then we'll head back for our afternoon training session."

All right! You are looking good out on the training field. Way to hang in there! Let's pray.

Now turn to page 163 and read 2 Timothy 3. Mark Paul by coloring him blue, color Timothy orange, and color all the other people pink. Don't forget to mark your pronouns!

Let's make a list on Paul.

WHAT I Learned About Paul

2 Timothy 3:11 Paul was _____ and _____ at _____, _____, and at _____. Paul e _ _ _ _ _ _ his persecutions, and the L _ _ _ _____ him.

Wow! Don't you want to be like Paul—able to endure all those persecutions and sufferings? Isn't it awesome to see that God rescued Paul out of all those persecutions!

Let's make a list on Timothy.

WHAT I Learned About Timothy

2 Timothy 3:10-11 Timothy followed Paul's

_____, _____, _____,

_____, _____, _____,

_____, _____ and _____.

2 Timothy 3:15 From c _ _ _ _ _ _ _ _ Timothy

has known the _____ _____ .

Did you know that right now you are becoming a "Timothy"? Timothy learned God's Word in childhood. That's what you are doing right now!

And just WHO are the other people in 2 Timothy 3? HOW are they described?

2 Timothy 3:2 Men who are _____ of

_____, lovers of _____, _____,

_____, _____, _____

to parents, _____, _____,

2 Timothy 3:3 _____, _____,

_____ gossips, without _____-

_____, _____, _____

of _____,

2 Timothy 3:4 _____, _____,

_____, lovers of _____ rather

than lovers of _____;

2 Timothy 3:5 holding to a form of _____,

although they have _____ its _____.

2 Timothy 3:6 They enter households and _____

weak _____.

2 Timothy 3:7 They are always _____ and

never able to come to the _____ of the

_____.

2 Timothy 3:8 They are like _____ and

_____, who opposed Moses. These

men _____ the _____, men of

_____ _____, rejected in regard to

the _____.

2 Timothy 3:9 They will not make further _____;

for their _____ will be _____ to all.

2 Timothy 3:13 _____ men and

_____ will proceed from _____

to _____, _____ and being

_____.

2 Timothy 3:5 WHAT does Paul tell Timothy to do?

_____

_____

Now, from the way these men are described, WHO are these men—believers in Jesus or unbelievers?

_____

Whew! Are you beginning to see WHY Paul is writing to Timothy? Think about what Paul keeps talking about, and think about these people you have been marking. If you don't see it right now, you will as you keep on studying. We are so proud of you! Keep up the good work. Tomorrow we will read the rest of Paul's letter to Timothy.

Now head back to the training field. Coach Neighbors is waiting to see just how many ankle jumps you can do while you say your verse.

DAY FIVE

GET READY TO RUN!

"Okay, team, today is our last day of practice. Tonight is the opening ceremony for our summer games, and then it will be time for the games to begin. Are you ready?"

"We're ready, Coach!" all the kids yelled out while Sam started jumping up and down, barking, and turning in circles.

Coach Neighbors laughed. "Looks like Sam is more than ready. Let's line up with our teams and rehearse tonight's opening."

"Great rehearsal! Max, why don't you lead everyone back inside and pray so we can wrap up our overview—the big picture on Paul's letter. Next week as we begin our games, we will start looking at the details."

"Yes, sir!" Max answered. "All right, let's head back to Hardaway Hall. Last one there has to give Sam a bath."

Immediately everyone started running. No one wants to bathe Sam—you know how he hates baths!

You made it! Thank heaven you ran so fast—now you won't have to bathe Sam. Today we are going to finish reading Paul's letter to get the big picture of WHY Paul wrote this letter to Timothy. Don't forget to ask God for His help.

Then turn to page 164 and read 2 Timothy 4. Mark Paul by coloring him blue, color Timothy orange, and color all the other people pink. Don't forget to mark your pronouns!

Let's make a list on Paul in the box below.

WHAT I Learned About Paul

2 Timothy 4:1 Paul _____ Timothy in the presence of _____ and _____ _____.

2 Timothy 4:6 Paul is being _____ out as a _____ _____. It is the time of Paul's _____.

2 Timothy 4:7 Paul has _____ the _____ _____, he has _____ the _____, he has kept the _____.

2 Timothy 4:8 In the future, Paul will receive the _____ of _____.

2 Timothy 4:10 Paul has been d __ __ __ __ __ __ __.

2 Timothy 4:11 Only _____ is with Paul. He wants Timothy to pick up and bring _____ with him.

2 Timothy 4:12 Paul sent _____ to _____.

2 Timothy 4:13 Paul left his _____ at Troas with Carpus. He wants Timothy to bring his c __ __ __ __, his _____, and especially the _____.

2 Timothy 2:14 _____ the coppersmith did Paul _____ _____.

2 Timothy 4:16 No one _____ Paul; all _____ him.

2 Timothy 4:17 The _____ stood with Paul and _____ Paul. Paul was _____ out of the _____ mouth.

Amazing! Paul's time to die has come, but he has been faithful to God. He has fought the good fight and finished the course even though he has suffered and been deserted by other people. Paul has gone for the gold! What about you? Don't you want to go for the gold too?

WHAT do we see about the other people in 2 Timothy 4:3-4?

The time will come when they will not _____ _____ _____. They will want to have their _____ _____. They will accumulate _____ in accordance with their own _____ and will _____ _____ their _____ from the _____ and will turn aside to _____.

2 Timothy 4:10 WHAT did Demas do?

_____

2 Timothy 4:14-15 WHAT about Alexander the copper-smith? WHAT did he do? _____

_____

Whoa, these men don't want to hear the truth! Instead, they turn aside from truth to myths. Demas loved the world, and Alexander did Paul harm. Have you noticed as we have read this letter that there are a lot of unfaithful people in the church and only a very few faithful ones? WHY do you think some stay faithful while others turn away? Could knowing God's Word, the truth, make a difference?

WHAT do you think? _____

_____

Now that we have read all of 2 Timothy, let's review what we have learned this week as we saw the big picture. Let's review by asking the 5 W's and an H questions.

WHO wrote the letter? _____

To WHOM was the letter written? _____

WHERE is Paul? _____

HOW is Paul being treated? _____

Look at 2 Timothy 1:8 and 2 Timothy 2:8-10. WHY is Paul in prison?

_____

2 Timothy 4:6 WHEN is this happening?

Paul says, "The time of my _____ has come."

Take a look at Max and Molly's notes below to gain more insight on what was happening at this time in history.

Nero the Roman Emperor

Nero was the Roman emperor at this time in history. Nero set a large majority of the city of Rome on fire and blamed the Christians in order to keep people from being suspicious of what he had done. He ordered Christians to be imprisoned and executed. Many Christians were put on poles alongside the highway and then, while they were still alive, they were set on fire to become human torches!

WHAT is the historical setting of this letter? WHAT is happening to Paul? Is this a time of persecution? Write out WHAT is happening at this time in history.

_____

WHAT did we learn about the other people that Paul talked about in his letter? Some were f __ __ __ __ __ __ __ men, and some were u __ __ __ __ __ __ __ __ __ __ men who turned away and opposed the truth. Do you think Paul might be warning Timothy about these unfaithful men in the church, men who teach things that aren't true?

Look back at 2 Timothy 3:5. WHAT did Paul tell Timothy to do?

A __ __ __ __ such _____ as these.

WHAT is the main thing 2 Timothy is about? Think about what Paul has repeated in his letter. Think about your memory verse too.

WHAT is Paul telling Timothy to do? _____

_____

_____

All right! You now have the big picture of Paul's letter to Timothy. You have discovered that Paul is writing to Timothy, his beloved son in the faith, because he is in prison, suffering for the gospel. Paul knows that he is about to die, so he is passing the baton on to Timothy. Do you know what it means to "pass the baton" on to someone? To pass the baton is to give the responsibility for something important to another person.

In a relay race, passing the baton is where one runner hands his baton to the next runner so the next runner can continue the race. Passing the baton is the most crucial part of the relay race. It is so important that track coaches spend hours training athletes how to transfer the baton from one runner to the next and continue the race at full speed. If the baton isn't passed inside the passing zone or it is dropped, the team will lose the race. The trick to winning the race is the passing of the baton.

Paul wants to help Timothy fulfill his responsibility to the gospel. Paul is passing the baton to Timothy, telling him to guard the treasure that has been entrusted to him.

How about you? Are you willing to take the baton of the gospel and pass it on to others? Do you know what the treasure, the gospel, is? You'll find out as we look at all the details in 2 Timothy 1 next week.

Don't forget your training to become God's champion. Say your memory verse out loud to some grown-ups this week. Ask them how they are guarding the treasure that has been entrusted to them.

2

DON'T BE ASHAMED

2 TIMOTHY 1

Wow! Wasn't that an awesome opening ceremony with all those cool fireworks? You did a fantastic job running in with the torch! Weren't you proud of Sam, all shiny and clean, wearing his USA bandana and walking so respectfully beside Max as he carried in the flag for the United States? It was so much fun watching all the kids walk in, representing different countries of the world and bringing us all together as one!

Last week as we began reading Paul's letter to Timothy, we got the big picture. This week we are going to start filling in the details so we can learn how to guard the treasure and become champions for God. We have opened the games, so let the competition begin!

DAY ONE

THE GAMES BEGIN!

"Run, Molly, run!" Max, Matthew, and Molly's other teammates yelled out as Molly took off out of the starting blocks.

"She did it!" Matthew high-fived Max. "Our first race, and Molly came in first place. Our first gold medal! Way to go, Molly!"

Wasn't that exciting? Now it's time to get back to our training in 2 Timothy. Don't forget to pray and thank God for giving you a strong mind and a healthy body to serve Him. Then ask Him to help you to understand His Word.

Fantastic! Today we are going to mark key words. What are key words? Key words are words that pop up more than once. They help unlock the meaning of the chapter or book you are studying and give you clues about what is most important in a passage of Scripture.

- Key words are usually used over and over again. (That's because God doesn't want you to miss the point.)

- Key words are important.

- Key words are used by the writer for a reason.

When you discover a key word, you need to mark it in a special way using a special color or symbol so you can immediately spot it in Scripture.

You may also want to make a bookmark for these key words

so you can see them at a glance as you mark them on your Observation Worksheets.

To make a key-word bookmark, get an index card or a piece of paper and write the key words listed below. Mark them with the colors and symbols you are going to use on your Observation Worksheets.

When you mark your key words, you will also need to mark any other words that mean the same thing, like pronouns or synonyms. You learned what pronouns were last week when you marked Paul and Timothy. Take a look at Molly and Max's training manual below to learn about synonyms.

Synonyms

Synonyms are different words that mean the same thing. *Sailboat*, *yacht*, and *rowboat* are all different words, but they all refer to boats. They are synonyms—ways to say the same thing with different words.

Great! Now, turn to page 160. Read 2 Timothy 1:1-7 and mark the key words and synonyms we have listed for you below.

God (Father, Lord) (draw a purple triangle and color it yellow)

Christ Jesus (and any other words that refer to Jesus, like *Lord*) (draw a purple cross and color it yellow)

remember (and the synonyms: recall, mindful, remind) (circle it in blue)

Don't forget to mark your pronouns! And mark anything that tells you WHEN by drawing a green clock or green circle like this: ○ .

All right! Now, let's ask the 5 W's and an H to solve the crossword puzzle below.

2 Timothy 1:2 HOW does Paul greet Timothy? WHAT does he say to Timothy, his beloved son?

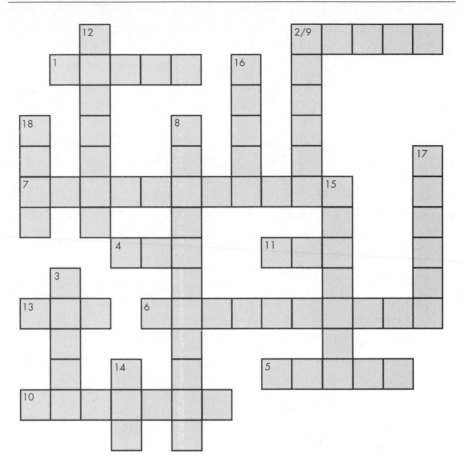

1. (Across) _____, 2. (Across) _____,
and 3. (Down)_____ from God the Father and
Christ Jesus our Lord.

2 Timothy 1:3 WHOM does Paul serve?

4. (Across) _____

2 Timothy 1:3 HOW does Paul serve God?

5. (Across) With a _____ 6. (Across) _____

2 Timothy 1:3 WHERE does Paul get his example? WHOM does Paul compare himself with?

7. (Across) His f __ __ __ __ __ __ __ __ __ __

2 Timothy 1:5 WHERE does Timothy get his example? WHERE did Timothy get his sincere faith?

8. (Down) His _____ Lois, and his

9. (Down) _____ Eunice.

Now, think about the things Paul is saying to Timothy. Do you know what Paul is doing? Paul is exhorting Timothy. An exhortation is an encouragement. An encouragement affirms us. It builds us up. An encouragement includes sincere and honest words of praise, like telling people how kind they are or that they are doing a great job.

Paul has a very important message for Timothy in his letter. But before Paul gives Timothy this message, Paul encourages and affirms Timothy.

Let's look at HOW Paul encourages Timothy.

Look at 2 Timothy 1:2 HOW does Paul encourage Timothy? WHAT does Paul call Timothy?

10. (Across) My _____ 11. (Across) _____

Wow! Paul reminds Timothy of his love and Timothy's importance to him. Timothy is his beloved son. Isn't it *awesome* when people remind you they love you and that you are special to them?

Turn to your Observation Worksheet on page 160 and draw a pink cloud around this encouragement: *Timothy, my beloved son.*

2 Timothy 1:3 HOW does Paul remember Timothy?

I constantly remember you in my 12. (Down) _____ night and day.

2 Timothy 1:4 WHAT is Paul longing for?

13. (Across) To _____ Timothy

2 Timothy 1:4 WHAT will seeing Timothy fill Paul with?

14. (Down) _____

Wouldn't it encourage you to know that someone close to you is praying for you, that they long to see you, and they are filled with joy when they see you?

Now draw a pink cloud around each one of these encouraging phrases on page 160.

2 Timothy 1:5 WHAT is Paul mindful of in Timothy?

15. (Down) His _____ 16. (Down) _____

Paul tells Timothy that he knows Timothy's faith is real! Don't you want people to be able to see that you have a faith that is real?

Draw a pink cloud around these encouraging words on page 160.

2 Timothy 1:6 WHAT is Paul's encouragement in this verse? WHAT is Paul reminding Timothy to do?

17. (Down) To _____ afresh the 18. (Down)

_____ of God.

Paul is reminding Timothy to "kindle afresh" the gift of God. To "kindle afresh" means to stir up his gift like stirring up the embers of a fire to get the fire blazing.

WHAT is this gift Paul is talking about? We'll find out tomorrow! For now, draw a pink cloud around these encouraging words on page 160.

You have done an awesome job reading Paul's letter and discovering how Paul encouraged Timothy, showing him how much he loved and prayed for Timothy and reminding him of his faith and his gift.

How about you? Can you encourage someone today? Maybe you can encourage a kid at school who doesn't have a lot of confidence, or a friend who is having a hard time. Sometimes kids are mean to other kids and make fun of them. You could encourage others by saying something nice to them to show them that they are special and valuable to God. Or you could encourage your mom or dad by telling them that you love them and are thankful for them.

Think of some people you can encourage today. Tell them how good they are at sports or art or something else. Remind them that you like to hang out with them. Write a note to your parents and tell them what a good job they are doing, what they mean to you, and how thankful you are for them. Reach out and show God's love by making someone feel special today!

Way to go! Before you head off to our next event in our summer games, let's see if you can solve this week's memory verse.

Look at the track on the next page. Follow the letters around the track. Begin at the start position. Cross out every other letter. Go from the inside track, following the arrows. When you finish, put the letters that remain on the blanks below to spell out your verse. Then look up 2 Timothy 1 and find the reference for this verse.

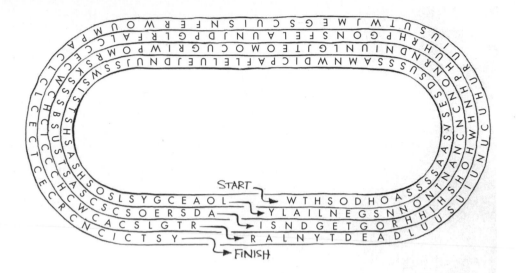

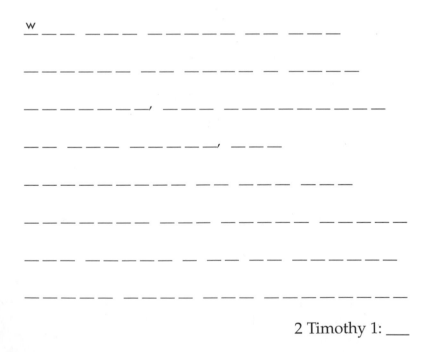

W _ _ _ _ _ _ _ _ _ _ _ _ _ _ _ _ _

_ _ _ _ _ _ _ _ _ _ _ _ _ _ _ _ _ _

_ _ _ _ _ _ _, _ _ _ _ _ _ _ _ _ _ _ _

_ _ _ _ _ _ _ _ _ _, _ _ _

_ _ _ _ _ _ _ _ _ _ _ _ _ _ _ _ _

_ _ _ _ _ _ _ _ _ _ _ _ _ _ _ _ _ _ _ _

_ _ _ _ _ _ _ _ _ _ _ _ _ _ _ _ _

_ _ _ _ _ _ _ _ _ _ _ _ _ _ _ _ _ _ _

2 Timothy 1: ___

Now write this verse out and practice saying it three times in a row out loud today!

DAY TWO

STRETCH...USE THAT GIFT FOR GOD

Hey, guys! Wasn't it an awesome day in our track and field events? That was one incredible long jump as you stretched out in the air to land the gold medal! Sam just can't wait to congratulate you with a good face licking!

Let's celebrate while we continue our training in 2 Timothy 1 so we can win the gold for God. Yesterday, as we opened Paul's letter to Timothy, we saw how Paul loved and encouraged Timothy. He reminded Timothy to kindle afresh the gift of God.

Today we need to find out HOW Paul encouraged Timothy to use his gift. But first, is Timothy the only one who has a gift? Let's find out. Don't forget to talk to God!

Let's look at some cross-references. Pull out your official Rulebook, your Bible, and look up 1 Peter 4:10-11.

1 Peter 4:10 WHAT does each one receive?

A _____ _____

1 Peter 4:10 HOW are we to use that gift?

To _____ one another as _____

_____ of the manifold grace of God.

1 Peter 4:11 WHY are we to use these gifts?

So that in _____ _____ _____

may be _____ through _____

_____.

Isn't that exciting? Timothy isn't the only one who gets a gift. God gives each one of us a gift when we accept Jesus Christ as our Savior.

But this gift isn't meant to make us feel good about ourselves. We are to use our gifts to serve one another and to bring God glory. Paul is encouraging Timothy to use the gift God has given Him.

HOW does Paul encourage Timothy to use this special gift? Turn to page 160 and read 2 Timothy 1:6-7. WHAT does Paul say to Timothy?

> 2 Timothy 1:7 WHAT has God *not* given us?
>
> A _____ of _____

That means we are not to be afraid. God has not given us a spirit of fear. We are not to fear man or what man can do to us.

HOW can we keep from being afraid? Look up and read Psalm 56:3-4.

> Psalm 56:3 WHAT does this verse tell us to do when we are afraid?
>
> _____

> Turn back to 2 Timothy 1:7 on page 160.
> WHAT has God given us?
>
> A spirit of _____ and _____ and
>
> _____

So HOW do we have power? Look up and read Acts 1:8.

> HOW do we receive power? WHERE do we get our
>
> power from? _____
>
> _____

Amazing! When we accept Jesus Christ as our Savior, the Holy Spirit comes and lives in us (John 14:23). And WHAT does He give us according to Acts 1:8?

P __ __ __ __ !

Acts 1:8 WHAT are we to be? Jesus' _____

Because we have power through the Holy Spirit, we can be witnesses about WHO Jesus is and WHAT He did for us. God gives us His power so we can share the good news about Jesus with other people.

WHAT else does 2 Timothy 1:7 tell us we have besides power?

L __ __ __ .

Look up and read 1 John 4:10-11.

WHAT did God do to show His love for us?

_____

What does the word *propitiation* mean? That's a big word, isn't it? When you think of propitiation, think of someone being satisfied, someone being appeased, someone else making amends for a wrong.

Another word for propitiation is *atonement*. Atonement is a covering for sin. In the Old Testament, people offered animal sacrifices to make an atonement to cover sin until the perfect sacrifice, Jesus Christ, came to earth as a baby to grow up, live a sinless life, and die on a cross to take away the sins of the whole world forever.

Sin separates us from God, but because God loves us, He gave His only Son, Jesus, to die on a cross and be the propitiation (atonement) for our sins. His blood doesn't just cover our sins; it takes them away forever and makes us right with God!

1 John 4:11 WHAT are we to do since God loves us?

_____

Read 1 John 4:18. WHAT do we see about love in this
verse?

_____

Because of God's great love and sacrifice for us, we do not
have to be afraid. Perfect love casts out fear. And because of
God's great love for us, we are to love others!

Now let's look at 2 Timothy 1:7 again and find the last thing
Paul tells Timothy God has given us. WHAT else has God given
us?

D _ _ _ _ _ _ _ _.

WHAT does this word mean? It means to have a sound mind,
to have self-control. It describes people who have their mind
under control. For example, suppose your mom makes you angry,
and you want to yell at her or slam the door to your room. But
instead of yelling or slamming your door, you decide to talk to
her in a respectful way. That's what it means to have your mind
under control. You want to say or do something hurtful, but you
don't. Think about it. An athlete has to train his mind. HOW can
we be disciplined? How can we have a steadfast mind?

Look up and read Isaiah 26:3.

HOW do we have a steadfast mind?

_____

Fantastic! You have seen Paul encourage Timothy to use his
gift by showing Timothy he has everything he needs. Timothy
has God's power, he has love, and he has a disciplined, steadfast
mind.

When you are afraid, remember that God loves you! You

can discipline your mind and keep it under control by putting your trust in God and His power. You can be loving and kind even when you don't want to, even when you are angry. God has given you power, love, and a sound mind, and you have the potential, the power to use those gifts!

DAY THREE

ON YOUR MARK...GET SET!

"All right, guys." Coach Neighbors called the relay team over. "Are you ready? It is almost time for our relay event. Matthew, remember that a good start is very important. That's why you're our first runner—you're great at getting out of the blocks and off to a quick start. Wes, you're a fast sprinter, and that's why you're next. Josh, you're a great curve runner, and Max, not only are you great under pressure, but you are fast, and we need that fighting spirit to bring that baton over the finish line first! Is everybody ready? Let's get loosened up, but first things first. We need to ask God to give us the strength to do our best and hang in there until the race is finished. Let's pray!"

While the guys are getting ready for the relay event, let's pull out our books. As we have looked at 2 Timothy 1 this week, we have seen that Paul opens his letter to Timothy by encouraging Timothy and affirming him, just as Coach Neighbors encouraged the guys to get them ready for their race. Let's find out WHAT else Paul says in his letter to Timothy.

Turn to page 160. Read 2 Timothy 1:8-14 and mark the key words and the synonyms we have listed for you below. Don't forget to add any new words to your key-word bookmark.

ashamed (draw a brown arch over it like this: ⌒)

gospel (Use the same symbol for any synonyms you

might see. A synonym is a another word that can take
the place of the word *gospel* and mean the same thing.
If you can put the word *gospel* in the place of this word,
then mark it. Here are some examples of synonyms for
gospel: *testimony of our Lord* (verse 8), *for which* (verse
11), *for this reason* (verse 12), *the standard of sound words*
(verse 13), and *treasure* (verse 14). Draw a red megaphone like this: and color it green.

suffering (suffer, chains) (draw a red squiggly line like
this:)

God (Father) (draw a purple triangle and color it
yellow)

Christ Jesus (and any other words that refer to Jesus,
like *Lord*) (draw a purple cross and color it yellow)

Holy Spirit (draw a purple and color it
yellow)

Don't forget to mark your pronouns! And mark anything that
tells you WHEN by drawing a green clock or green circle
like this: .

Awesome! Did you notice that after Paul encourages Timothy, he gives Timothy some instructions on what Timothy needs to do? An instruction is a specific "do this" or "don't do that" command. Ask the 5 W's and an H to discover WHAT Paul tells Timothy to do.

2 Timothy 1:8 WHAT is the first thing we see Paul telling Timothy *not* to do? _____

_____

WHAT does Paul mean when he tells Timothy not to be ashamed of the testimony of our Lord? Being ashamed is like feeling so embarrassed or humiliated that you don't tell someone about Jesus. The phrase "testimony of our Lord" means a witness of Jesus. (Remember, in this passage, this phrase is a synonym that can replace the word *gospel*.) Paul is telling Timothy not to be embarrassed of the gospel of Jesus or of him, the Lord's prisoner.

Have you ever felt embarrassed to tell someone about Jesus? _____ WHY? WHAT did you think would happen? _____

_____

HOW do you think Jesus feels about that?

_____

Pull out your official Rulebook, your Bible. Look up and read Mark 8:38 to see WHAT Jesus says about being ashamed of Him.

Mark 8:38 WHAT will the Son of Man be to the person who is ashamed of Jesus and His words?

The _____ of _____ will also be

_____ of him when He _____ in

the glory of His Father with the holy angels.

Look up and read Matthew 10:32-33.

Matthew 10:33 WHAT happens if we deny Jesus before

men? _____

_____

Whoa! That means that if we are ashamed of Jesus and His words while we are living on this earth, He will be ashamed of us when He comes back! He will deny us before God!

Think about that. Have you ever been ashamed of Jesus? Write out what you did or didn't do.

_____

_____

Look back at 2 Timothy 1:8. WHAT else does Paul tell Timothy to do?

_____

Ouch! That doesn't sound like a lot of fun does it?

2 Timothy 1:8 HOW are we able to suffer like Paul? WHAT does God give us? The p __ __ __ r of God!

Look up and read 1 Corinthians 10:13. HOW is God faithful?

_____

_____

_____

Suffering isn't fun, but it's part of being a believer in Jesus. When we love and serve Jesus, there will be times of suffering and persecution. Sometimes we will suffer when we don't want to let God run our lives, when we don't want Him to have first place. And sometimes we will suffer and be persecuted because of our testimony of believing in Jesus and sharing the gospel with others. People will make fun of us or hurt us. But God is faithful. God will give us a way out of our suffering, or He will give us strength and His power to endure it!

Let's put a green box around each one of the instructions that Paul gives Timothy. Turn to page 160 and put a green box around the instructions *do not be ashamed of the testimony of our Lord or of me His prisoner* and *join with me in suffering for the gospel.*

Do you see any other instructions in verses 8-14? How about in 2 Timothy 1:13? WHAT is Paul's instruction?

_____

2 Timothy 1:14 WHAT does Paul tell Timothy to do?

_____

HOW are you to guard the treasure?

Through the _____ _____ who

_____ in _____.

Wow, the Holy Spirit is going to help you!

Turn to page 161 and draw a green box around each of these instructions in verses 13-14.

Now, WHAT is each one of these instructions to Timothy about? Look at each instruction that you put a green box around on page 161. WHAT is the key word you marked in each of these instructions?

_____

Amazing! Each one of these instructions is about the gospel! Let's make a list in the box below by looking at each place we marked *gospel* or any synonyms for the gospel in 2 Timothy 1 on our Observation Worksheet.

WHAT I Learned About the Gospel

2 Timothy 1:8 Do _____ be _____ of the _____ of our _____.

2 Timothy 1:8 Join with me in _____ for the gospel.

2 Timothy 1:10 The appearing of our _____ _____ _____, who abolished _____ and brought _____ and _____ to _____ through the gospel.

2 Timothy 1:11 Paul was appointed a _____ and an _____ and a _____ for the gospel.

2 Timothy 1:12 Paul _____ for the gospel but was not _____.

2 Timothy 1:13 _____ the _____ of _____ _____ (the gospel).

2 Timothy 1:14 _____ the _____ (the gospel) which has been _____ to you.

Wow! Think about what these verses show us about the gospel. We are not to be ashamed of it. We are to suffer for it. It is revealed through Jesus; it is the reason that Paul is a preacher, an apostle, and a teacher; we are to retain it and guard it; the gospel has been entrusted to us!

You have learned a lot of things about the gospel today, but do you know WHAT the gospel is? Here's a hint. Take a look at verse 10 on your list. Tomorrow you will find out WHAT the gospel is and see WHAT God and Jesus have done for you! You have done a great job! Don't forget to practice your memory verse.

DAY FOUR

PASS THE BATON!

"Great, Matthew, way to go!" Coach Neighbors yelled out as he watched Matthew run in, hit the go mark, and hand the baton off to Wes. "Run, Wes, run! Good, good…now pass that baton to Josh. You got it, Josh! Way to take that curve! Uh-oh…hang in there…get that baton to Max—you can do it. All right, Max, pour it on! You can handle the pressure…push, Max, push!

"Yeah! You did it! Way to go, guys! Way to go, Josh! You didn't let that turn of the ankle stop you. Way to hang in there and get that baton to Max. You guys are awesome!"

How about that? The guys hung in there. Josh pressed through his pain when he turned his ankle, he was able to hand off the baton to Max, and Max pressed on to win the race! Man, that is so awesome!

Let's find out how we can pass on the baton of the gospel. But before we can pass it on, we need to be sure we know WHAT the gospel is. Don't forget to pray! Then turn to page 160 and read 2 Timothy 1:8–10.

WHAT is the gospel? Let's ask the 5 W's and an H.

2 Timothy 1:9 WHAT did God do for us?

He _____ us and _____ us with

a _____ _____.

2 Timothy 1:9 HOW did God save us?

Not _____ to our _____ but

according to His own _____ and _____

which was _____ to us in _____

_____ from all _____.

Let's think this through. Grace is something you don't earn. It is something you don't deserve. Grace is a free gift, a total gift.

So are we saved by works—the things we do—or by God's grace—His free gift?

_____

_____

WHOM is this granted in? _____

_____

Wow! We can do absolutely nothing to save ourselves. It is only through the grace of God. Being saved comes from believing and trusting in Christ Jesus.

2 Timothy 1:10 WHAT did our Savior Christ Jesus do to death?

Jesus _____ death!

HOW did Jesus abolish death? Let's read 1 Corinthians 15:1-8 (printed out below) and mark the following key words:

gospel (and any synonyms, like *which* and *the word*) (draw a red megaphone like this: and color it green)

Christ (draw a purple cross and color it yellow)

Don't forget to mark your pronouns!

1 Corinthians 15:1-8

1 Now I make known to you, brethren, the gospel which I preached to you, which also you received, in which also you stand, **2** by which also you are saved, if you hold fast the word which I preached to you, unless you believed in vain.

3 For I delivered to you as of first importance what I also received, that Christ died for our sins according to the Scriptures, and that He was buried, **4** and that He was raised on the third day according to the Scriptures, **5** and that He appeared to Cephas, then to the twelve. **6** After that He appeared to more than five hundred brethren at one time, most of whom remain until now, but some have fallen asleep; **7** then He appeared to James, then to all the apostles; **8** and last of all, as to one untimely born, He appeared to me also.

1 Corinthians 15:1 WHAT is Paul making known to them? WHAT is he preaching? The _____

1 Corinthians 15:2-4 WHAT is the gospel? HOW are you saved? WHAT do you have to believe?

_____ died for our _____ according to the _____ and that He was _____, and that He was _____ on the _____ day according to the _____.

**The first point of the gospel
is that Jesus died for our sins.**

1 Corinthians 15:3 says that Jesus died for our sins according to the Scriptures. This means that Jesus' dying for our sins was written about in the Old Testament before He ever came to earth as a baby. Jesus came to earth as a human being, but He was still God. This is called the *incarnation*. *Incarnation* is a big word that means being or taking flesh. It is God becoming human. Jesus was God in the flesh. This is a very important doctrine (teaching) that is essential to the gospel.

Jesus was different from all other human beings because He was not born a sinner. God was His Father. Although Jesus was tempted like we are, Jesus never sinned. He always obeyed His Father, and because he never sinned, He could pay for our sins.

Jesus' death on the cross was the propitiation (atonement) for our sins. Remember what we learned about propitiation on day 2? *Propitiation* means that God was satisfied with Jesus' payment for our sins.

WHY would Jesus need to pay for our sins? WHAT does sin cause? Look up and read Romans 6:23.

Romans 6:23 WHAT is the wages of sin?

_____

WHAT is the free gift of God?

_____

Because sin brings death and would separate us from God forever, God in His love for us gave His only Son, Jesus, to die on a cross and to be the propitiation (atonement) for our sins so that we could be with God forever.

Think about it. Jesus, who had never sinned, did not deserve to die, but He chose to take our place and die on the cross to pay for our sin. He was our substitute. His death took away our sins so that we can have the free gift of eternal life! Isn't that incredible!

Look back at 1 Corinthians 15:3 printed out on page 53.

WHAT did people do with Jesus' body after He died?

_____

WHY do you bury someone? Because they are dead! So if Jesus was buried, was He really dead? __Yes __ No

Is that good news—that Jesus was dead? No! So if dying isn't good news, WHERE is the good news? Look back at 1 Corinthians 15:4 on page 53.

WHAT did Jesus do on the third day?

_____

**The second point of the gospel
is that Jesus was buried and resurrected.**

The good news is that even though Jesus died and was buried, He didn't stay dead—He was raised on the third day!!

HOW do we know that Jesus was raised from the dead? Look at 1 Corinthians 15:5-8.

1 Corinthians 15:5 WHAT did Jesus do?

_____

1 Corinthians 15:6-8 HOW many others did Jesus appear to?

_____

Do you know WHO the "me" is in verse 8? That's Paul. Jesus appeared to Paul too! Isn't this *amazing*? We know that even though Jesus died, He didn't stay dead. He was raised on the third day! Death could not hold Jesus. Jesus was resurrected—that's how Jesus abolished death and gives us life and immortality. *Immortality* means we will live forever!

So, WHAT is the gospel? The Greek word for *gospel* is *euangelion*. It is pronounced like this: *yoo-ang-ghel-ee-on*. The word *gospel* means "good news." It's the good news that Jesus paid the penalty for our sins. Remember, the payment for sin is death. Sinners have to die, but Jesus didn't *have* to die because He didn't sin. Jesus took our place and *voluntarily* died on the cross so He could pay for our sin! We can't do anything to save ourselves. We can never ever be good enough. Being good does not take away our sins. Jesus is the only one who can take away sin.

Let's look up and read John 14:6.

WHAT does Jesus say? "I am the _____, and the _____, and the _____; _____ _____comes to the _____but through _____."

WOW! Jesus tells us He is the only way to God! And *no one*—Gentiles, Jews, Hindus, Muslims, Buddhists, or churchgoers—

can get to God without believing in Jesus. Jesus is the *only* way to God and heaven.

This is the gospel. This is the standard of sound words we are to keep and never turn away from, according to 2 Timothy 1:13. This is the treasure we are to guard. It never changes, and it never will. This is why Paul is a prisoner. He believed the gospel. He guarded the truth of it. That's why Paul suffered. Athletes must endure physical suffering and lots of discipline to become champions in their sport, and we must endure suffering and discipline ourselves to become true champions for God.

So HOW do you become God's champion? HOW do you accept Jesus Christ as your Savior and receive eternal life? The first thing you need to do is know WHO Jesus is. You have to believe that Jesus is God's Son, that He is God, and that as a man He lived a perfect life without sin and died on a cross to pay for our sins. Then He was buried, and God raised Him from the dead. He is the *only* Savior!

You have to believe you are a sinner and that you need someone to save you because you can't save yourself. You have to be willing to confess to God that you are a sinner and turn away from your sin (repent). You have to be willing to turn your entire life over to God, to become a follower of Jesus Christ.

If you truly believe in WHO Jesus is and WHAT He did for you, and if you know you are a sinner who cannot save yourself, then you are ready to receive Jesus as your Savior.

To believe in Jesus means you are willing to turn away from doing things your way and to begin obeying Jesus. Jesus puts it this way. You have to be willing to deny yourself, take up your cross (die to being your own God), and follow Him (Mark 8:34).

An athlete has to submit to his coach and learn. In the same way, when you truly believe in Jesus, you are willing to submit to Him and let Him be your Coach, your Boss, your Lord, your Ruler, your God. You have to be willing to let Jesus have complete control over your life.

Take some time and think about what you have learned about WHO Jesus is and WHAT He has done for you. Ask yourself, *Am I ready to give my life to Jesus and let Him take over my life?*

It's a big decision, so think about what it really means. If you aren't sure you understand, you can talk with a grown-up.

All right! Now that you know what the gospel is and how you can receive it, with WHOM can you share the good news about Jesus? _____

_____

Way to go! Now practice your memory verse, and as you say it out loud, think about HOW *awesome* God is and WHAT He has done for you!

DAY FIVE

FINISH STRONG!

Hey, guys, it's great to have you back on the field for the last day of our track and field events. Are your ready to run a mile for Team USA? It'll take a lot of endurance, but we know you can do it! Sam will run alongside you to encourage you as you run.

What a race! You won a silver medal. All right! But it could have been gold if you hadn't turned away to look at your opponent. Remember to keep your eyes on the finish line.

Now, catch your breath while you talk to God. Let's head back to 2 Timothy 1. Turn to page 161 and read 2 Timothy 1:15–18. Mark the key words and synonyms listed below.

ashamed (turned away) (draw a brown arch over it like this: ⌒)

God (Father, Lord) (draw a purple triangle and color it yellow)

Don't forget to mark anything that tells you WHERE by double underlining the WHERE in green. Mark anything that tells you WHEN by drawing a green clock 🕐 or green circle like this: ◯ .

Now, ask those 5 W's and an H to find out who is and who isn't ashamed of the gospel.

2 Timothy 1:15 WHO turned away from Paul?

_____

Are you surprised to see that these people turned away, were ashamed of Paul? Do you think that these who are ashamed of Paul are also ashamed of the gospel?

_____

Are they true believers if they are ashamed? _____

From WHAT we have learned, will Jesus confess or deny them? _____

_____

2 Timothy 1:16 WHO was not ashamed of Paul?

_____

2 Timothy 1:16 WHAT did Onesiphorus do for Paul?

_____

2 Timothy 1:17 WHAT did Onesiphorus do when he
was in Rome? _____

2 Timothy 1:18 WHAT did Paul ask the Lord to grant
Onesiphorus?

_____

Have you noticed how sometimes kids will be part of a team
for a little while but will quit (turn away) when they don't like
the coach or the coach is too demanding? Onesiphorus didn't
turn away. He was faithful to Paul.

Let's match the people we have met in 2 Timothy 1 in the left
column on the next page to the words in the right column by
drawing lines to show whether they are ashamed or not ashamed
of the gospel.

Think about the things you learned about each one of these
people as you studied 2 Timothy 1. For an example, WHAT did
you learn about Timothy as you made your lists last week? You
saw that Timothy has proven worth, and he has been faithful in
serving with Paul in furthering the gospel. So would Timothy be
ashamed or not ashamed of the gospel?

_____

Now draw a line from each person's name to show whether
they are ashamed or not ashamed of the gospel according to
what you have learned about them.

Paul	ashamed
Timothy	ashamed
All those in Asia	not ashamed
Phygelus	not ashamed
Hermogenes	not ashamed
Onesiphorus	ashamed
_____	_____

In the last blank under Onesiphorus' name write your name. Take a moment and ask yourself WHOM you are most like—Paul, Timothy, those in Asia, or Onesiphorus. Then write whom you are most like and what describes you—not ashamed or ashamed of the gospel.

Way to go! You have done an outstanding job this week! Just look at all you have learned. You know how very important the gospel is. You know the gospel is revealed through Jesus, and believing the gospel is the only way you can have eternal life. You know that you are not to be ashamed of it. You know you are to be willing to suffer for it. The gospel is a treasure. You are to keep the truth of it. You are to guard it and share it with others. Awesome! We are so proud of you!

Now take that baton of the gospel and run hard, run fast, and hand it off to your family and friends. Persevere until the race is won! And don't forget to say your memory verse out loud to a grown-up.

3

ENTRUST TO FAITHFUL MEN

2 TIMOTHY 2:1-13

Last week was incredible as we began competing in our summer games and saw HOW Paul encouraged Timothy in his letter. Paul reminded Timothy of his love for him, the faith they share, and Timothy's need to stir up the gift God gave him. We also saw Paul give Timothy some instructions on his responsibility to the gospel of Jesus Christ. We discovered not only WHAT the gospel is but also HOW important it is for us to pass the gospel on to others.

WHAT will we discover this week? Let's find out.

DAY ONE

BE STRONG!

"Okay, guys." Coach Neighbors gathered the kids together at Hardaway Hall. "You did a great job for Team USA in our track and field events. Tomorrow will begin our swimming and diving events. Girls, the first events are yours. Are you ready to swim for the gold?"

Molly and all the girls gave a loud shout. "All right then!"

Coach smiled. "Let's get our minds prepared by working on 2 Timothy. Molly, why don't you pray so we can see what else Paul has to say to Timothy."

Turn to page 161. Read 2 Timothy 2:1-2 and mark the key words and synonyms listed below.

Christ Jesus (and any other words that refer to Jesus, like *Lord*) (draw a purple cross and color it yellow)

gospel (and synonyms for the gospel: *the things which you have heard from me*, and *these* [both in verse 2]) (draw a red megaphone like this: ◁ and color it green)

Fantastic! Let's ask the 5 W's and an H to discover Paul's instructions to Timothy.

2 Timothy 2:1 WHAT does Paul tell Timothy to do?

_____

2 Timothy 2:1 WHERE will Timothy get the strength to do what Paul tells him to do? _____

_____

Turn to page 161 and draw a green box around the instruction that Paul gives Timothy in 2 Timothy 2:1.

2 Timothy 2:2 WHAT are "the things which you have heard"?

The g _ _ _ _ _

2 Timothy 2:2 WHAT is Paul's instruction about the gospel?

_____

2 Timothy 2:2 WHY did Paul say Timothy was to entrust the gospel to faithful men? WHAT kind of men

did we see in 2 Timothy 1:15, faithful men or unfaith-

ful?_____

2 Timothy 1:16-18 HOW about Onesiphorus—was he

faithful or unfaithful? _____

_____

2 Timothy 2:2 WHAT will these faithful men be able to
do?

_____

Turn to page 159. Draw a green box around the instruction
that Paul gives Timothy in 2 Timothy 2:2.

To be able to teach someone God's Word, you have to learn it
yourself. You're doing that right now! But it doesn't stop there.
You need not only to know it but also to help others learn it. And
HOW do you do that? One way you can teach others is to ask
your friends if they would like to do one of these Bible studies
with you. Do you know of someone you could ask to do a study
with you? Write his or her name here: _____ .

Pray and ask God to give your friends the desire to study His
Word with you, and ask Him to help you show them how to see
truth for themselves.

All right! You are doing great! Take a look at the swimming
pool on the next page to solve your memory verse. Each of the
swimming lanes contains different words. Some of these words
have to do with swimming. Look at each word, and if it has to do
with swimming, put an X over it. Then write all the unmarked
words on the blanks underneath to solve your verse. Read
2 Timothy 2 to find the reference for this verse.

Be	swim	diligent	flip	to
Freestyle	present	yourself	stroke	approved
pull	kick	to	God	glide
as	a	butterfly	workman	water
who	does	backstroke	not	need
to	dolphin kick	be	backstroke	ashamed
accurately	racing	handling	the	spin turn
Word	breathe	of	breaststroke	truth.

_____ _____ _____ _____

_____ _____ _____ _____

_____ _____ _____ _____ _____

_____ _____ _____ _____ _____,

_____ _____ _____ _____

_____ _____ _____.

2 Timothy 2: _____

Now, write this verse out and practice saying it out loud three times in a row!

DAY TWO

COMPETE TO WIN

"Molly, Katie, Morgan, and Bethany, it's almost time for the 400-meter freestyle relay," Coach Neighbors told the girls as they gathered at the pool. "Now, just remember the rules," he continued. "Don't forget to touch the wall so the next swimmer can dive in, and make sure you don't dive into the pool until your teammate has touched the wall, or you will be disqualified. Remember, you disqualify yourself when you don't follow the rules. Are you girls ready? Shake those arms to loosen up."

While the girls are warming up for their event, let's work on our letter from Paul. Pray and ask God to help you to be strong and entrust the gospel to others.

All right! Now, turn to page 161. Read 2 Timothy 2:3-6 and mark the key words listed below (and any synonyms).

suffering (suffer, chains) (draw a red squiggly line like this: ~~~~)

Christ Jesus (and any other words that refer to Jesus, like *Lord*) (draw a purple cross and color it yellow)

Ask the 5 W's and an H to discover Paul's instruction and the examples he gives Timothy.

2 Timothy 2:3 WHAT is Paul's instruction to Timothy?

_____ _____ with me.

Turn to page 161 and draw a green box around the instruction that Paul gives Timothy.

2 Timothy 2:3 HOW does Paul tell Timothy to suffer hardship with him? WHAT is his example?

Like a good _____ of _____

_____ .

2 Timothy 2:4 WHAT do we learn about the soldier? WHAT kind of service is he in? _____

_____

2 Timothy 2:4 WHAT doesn't the soldier in active service do?

_____ himself in the _____

of _____ _____ .

2 Timothy 2:4 WHAT does the soldier want to do?

_____ the one who _____ him

as a soldier.

A good soldier knows he is to give his undivided allegiance to please the one he serves. He does not get caught up in everyday life. He knows his duties, and he keeps his focus on what he is called to do. A good soldier never runs away from the front lines, even when the battle is fierce. He stands his ground and continues to fight because of something he is willing to suffer for, something worth living and dying for.

Do you want to be a good soldier? Is it the desire of your heart to please God? _____. Write out one way you can please God. _____

WHAT can you do to keep yourself from getting caught up in the world you live in? Will you be careful about the clothes you wear, the music you listen to, and the movies you see so that you please God and not your friends? Write out WHAT you will do to keep yourself from getting entangled in this world.

_____

_____

Now, what is the next example that Paul gives us? Look at 2 Timothy 2:5 WHAT is our example?

An _____

2 Timothy 2:5 WHAT do we learn about the athlete?

He does not _____ the _____ unless

he competes according to the _____.

How about that? An athlete's life is about obedience. If he doesn't follow the rules, he won't get the prize. Remember what Coach Neighbors told the girls about touching the wall.

Look up and read 1 Corinthians 9:24-27.

1 Corinthians 9:24 WHAT is the athlete to do?

_____ in such a way that you may _____.

1 Corinthians 9:25 WHAT does the one who competes in the games have to exercise? _____-_____ in all things.

An athlete's life is about self-control and obedience. He disciplines his body so he can compete in the games. If he doesn't obey the rules, he will be disqualified, and he won't win the prize! Don't you want to be the best you can be for God? Write out a way you will discipline yourself. HOW will you obey God?

_____

_____

Did you also notice that 1 Corinthians 9:25 says the athlete wins a perishable prize, one that won't last, but we receive an imperishable prize, one that lasts forever? In 2 Timothy 4:7-8 we read about a reward for finishing the course. Did you know that there are rewards for loving and serving God? Look up and read Revelation 22:12.

Revelation 22:12 WHAT does Jesus have with Him when He comes?

His _____

WHOM is He going to give this to?

Every _____ according to what he has _____

Wow! Even though we are saved by grace and not by the things we do, the things we do are important. Our actions don't save us, but they show that we love and serve God. One day we will receive a reward!

Let's look at our last example.

2 Timothy 2:6 WHOM does Paul give us as an example?

The _____-_____ _____

2 Timothy 2:6 WHAT will he be the first to receive?

His _____ of the _____

The farmer works hard. He has to get up early to plow, sow, tend, and reap his harvest. He has trials—like bugs, frost, and droughts—that can destroy his crops. But a farmer who works hard and endures will reap a harvest.

Are you willing to work hard for God? _____

WHAT are some trials you might face as you serve Him?

_____

Do you know any kids who don't have to work for anything, who don't have any responsibilities? We are to be like the farmer. We are to work hard and endure. Being a Christian is not a free ride.

If you share the Word (plant the seed) so others can know about Jesus, and if you endure by working hard, being faithful, and not giving up, you will get to share in the harvest, just as the farmer does. Remember, Jesus is coming back one day soon, and His reward is with Him. Will you hang in there and endure so you can reap a harvest?

Aren't these awesome examples? Paul has mentioned the good soldier, the athlete, and the farmer to show us that becoming a champion for God requires suffering, undivided allegiance, self-discipline, obedience, hard work, and endurance.

Don't forget to practice your memory verse!

Day Three
Receive the Prize

Max, Matthew, Wes, and Josh all cheered as the girls lined up on the platform to receive their prize for the 400-meter freestyle relay. "Way to go, girls, you did great!" They whistled and clapped as each girl was awarded a gold medal.

Aren't you proud of our awesome team? Those girls disciplined themselves to keep their cool under all that pressure. They worked so hard and didn't give up, and now just look—they have won gold medals! Remember, if we don't work, we won't receive a reward.

How about you? Are you ready to work hard so you can receive God's reward? Don't forget to ask God for His help so you can discipline yourself to please Him.

Now, turn to page 162. Read 2 Timothy 2:7-10 and mark the key words listed below (and any synonyms).

God (Father) (draw a purple triangle and color it yellow)

Christ Jesus (and any other words that refer to Jesus, like *Lord*) (draw a purple cross and color it yellow)

gospel (and synonyms for the gospel: *for which, the word of God* [verse 9], *for this reason* [verse 10]) (draw a red megaphone like this: and color it green)

suffering (suffer, chains) (draw a red squiggly line like this:)

2 Timothy 2:7 WHAT is Paul's next instruction?

_____ what I _____.

Paul wants Timothy to think on these things.

Turn to page 162 and draw a green box around this instruction.

> 2 Timothy 2:7 WHEN you consider what Paul says, when you think on these things, WHAT will the Lord give you?
>
> _____ in everything

> 2 Timothy 2:8 WHAT is the next instruction?
>
> _____ _____ _____.

Turn to page 162 and draw a green box around this instruction.

> 2 Timothy 2:8 WHY are we to remember? WHAT did
>
> Jesus do for us? Jesus Christ is _____ from the
>
> _____.

Jesus conquered death for us!

> 2 Timothy 2:8 WHO is Jesus?
>
> A _____ of _____

> 2 Timothy 2:9 Even though we are suffering and even imprisoned, WHAT is not imprisoned?
>
> The _____ _____ _____

> 2 Timothy 2:10 WHY is Paul enduring all things?
>
> For the g __ __ __ __ __, for the sake of those who
>
> are _____, so that they may obtain
>
> _____

Way to go! God's Word is never imprisoned. We are to be like a good soldier, athlete, and farmer. We are to give God first place, please Him, obey His commands, suffer hardship, and endure so that others may receive salvation in Christ Jesus!

Now go back and find all the words in each blank starting on page 68 on day 2 and going through today's questions (not including your application questions) and circle each one of these words in the word search below. (If a word is used more than once, circle it just one time.)

You have done an outstanding job! What a way to please God!

U	N	D	E	R	S	T	A	N	D	i	N	G	C	L
D	A	V	i	D	E	T	S	i	L	N	E	S	i	R
P	T	W	Z	E	L	G	N	A	T	N	E	F	R	L
R	H	N	H	H	F	Y	A	D	Y	R	E	V	E	E
i	L	E	A	E	C	i	V	R	E	S	U	W	D	P
Z	E	S	R	D	O	E	R	A	H	S	X	N	i	S
E	T	O	D	O	N	O	i	T	A	V	L	A	S	O
R	E	H	S	G	T	E	E	W	O	R	K	i	N	G
U	S	C	H	F	R	N	C	R	E	i	D	L	O	S
L	A	O	i	O	O	Y	A	S	P	R	G	D	C	R
E	E	i	P	D	L	R	E	M	E	M	B	E	R	i
S	L	C	H	R	i	S	T	M	H	D	j	A	O	A
L	P	K	L	O	B	D	R	A	W	E	R	D	P	F
Z	V	N	i	W	H	A	R	D	j	E	S	U	S	F
Z	W	S	U	F	F	E	R	P	E	V	i	T	C	A

DAY FOUR
DIVE INTO TRUTH

Amazing! That was smoothest dive we have ever seen you do. You sliced right into that pool with hardly a splash! Another gold medal for Team USA! Wasn't it a little bit nerve-racking as you climbed up each one of those steps and looked off the diving platform? All that training sure paid off. Why don't you dry off so we can find out about a trustworthy statement Paul mentions in his letter. Don't forget to pray!

Turn to page 162 so we can dive into God's Word. Read 2 Timothy 2:11-13 and mark the following key word.

Christ Jesus (draw a purple cross and color it yellow)

Now, ask the 5 W's and an H.

2 Timothy 2:11 WHAT is this statement?

A _____ statement

That means that it is a true statement. WHAT is the first part of this true statement in 2 Timothy 2:11?

For if we _____ with _____

2 Timothy 2:11 WHO is the *Him*? Look back at verse 10 to see WHO this *Him* is. Salvation is in WHOM? _____

_____

Look up and read Romans 6:3-10.

Romans 6:6 WHAT do we see about our old self?

_____

WHY? In order that our body of _____ might be done away with, so that we would no longer be _____ to _____.

To die with Christ is to surrender our lives to Jesus by accepting Jesus as our Lord and Savior, confessing our sin, and changing the way we live. We have died to our old self. We are no longer slaves to sin. By dying to sin, we identify ourselves with Jesus' death.

So, WHAT is the second part of the true statement?

2 Timothy 2:11 WHAT happens if we die with Christ?

We will _____ with Him.

Look back at Romans 6:9-10.

Romans 6:9 WHAT do we see about Christ?

_____

Romans 6:9 WHAT do we see about death?

_____

Isn't that *awesome*? Because Jesus was resurrected, death no longer has any hold on Him. And when we identify ourselves with Jesus and give Him our lives, death doesn't have a hold on us either! When we die, we will be raised—just like Jesus—to live with Him forever!

Look at Romans 6:10 WHAT did Christ do?

He _____ to _____ once for all; but the _____ that He _____, He _____ to _____.

Did you catch this last part in verse 10? HOW does Christ live?

_____

Because Jesus gave up His life for us, we will live with Jesus forever! Isn't that exciting! We have been saved from our death and sin, and now we are to live our lives for God!

Are you doing that? Think about HOW you spend your time. Write out HOW you spend your time every day.

_____

_____

Do these things show that you are living your life for God, or are these just things you want to do?

_____

HOW can you live your life for God? WHAT kinds of things do you think God would like you to spend your time doing?

_____

Do you ask God how you can live for Him? Write out a prayer to God on the lines below and ask Him HOW you can live your life for Him. _____

_____

_____

_____

HOW can you give your best to God? Could God want you to be willing to reach out and serve other people to show His love to them? Read each one of the statements below and put a checkmark by the ones you will do.

- I will reach out and be a friend to someone in my school or at church who is shy or needs a friend. _____
- I will work hard at school and do my best instead of goofing off and just getting by. _____

- I will use my talents to play sports, a musical instrument, or serve others. _____

- I will help my mom and dad at home. _____

- I will help someone else, like a neighbor or an older lady who may need help working in her yard, cutting grass, or cleaning house. _____

All right! Think about the talents you have and use them for God. Tomorrow we will continue to look at the trustworthy statements that Paul tells Timothy about. Don't forget to practice your memory verse!

DAY FIVE

ENDURE TO THE END

"Sam, come back here. Sam, don't you jump in that pool!" Max yelled out as he chased Sam. "Hey, Molly, run around the pool on the other side. Let's see if we can catch Sam before he hits the water."

Splash! Too late. Sam, you are one bad dog! What are we ever going to do with you? Why don't you dry Sam off so Max and

Matthew get can get ready for the boys' last swimming event. Grab your towel and your book, and let's head back to 2 Timothy 2. Don't forget to pray.

Turn to page 162 and read 2 Timothy 2:11-13. WHAT is the next part of the true statement that Paul makes to Timothy?

2 Timothy 2:12 WHAT happens if we endure?

_____

Look up and read James 1:12.

WHAT will the man receive who perseveres under a trial?

_____

Look up and read Revelation 20:4-6.

Revelation 20:6 WHAT do we see about those who have a part in the first resurrection. WHAT will they be?

_____ of God and of _____

WHAT will they do?

_____

Isn't that amazing? If we hang in there and persevere, one day we will reign with Christ! Christianity isn't for quitters! Let's look at the next part of our true statement.

2 Timothy 2:12 WHAT happens if we deny Jesus?

_____

HOW can we deny Jesus? Look up and read Titus 1:16.

Titus 1:16 WHAT do they profess?

_____

Titus 1:16 HOW do they deny God?

_____

Titus 1:16 HOW are they described?

_____

WOW! Once again we see that the things we do show whether or not we really know God. Are you obedient or disobedient?

_____

WHAT are your deeds? WHAT are the things you do that show that you love and serve God? _____

_____

Look at 2 Timothy 2:13 WHAT happens if we are faithless?

_____

WHY will He remain faithful?

_____

God is soooooo *awesome*! Even when we lack faith and are unfaithful, He is still faithful! God is always true to Himself. Isn't that exciting? We can always trust God because He is ALWAYS faithful. God always acts according to His character and His promises.

You have learned so much this week in 2 Timothy 2, and we aren't even finished yet. Don't forget to say your memory verse to a grown-up. This is a very important verse that we will take a closer look at next week. Now, go celebrate Max and Matthew's great 100-meter swim!

4

HANDLE GOD'S WORD ACCURATELY

2 TIMOTHY 2:14-26

Wasn't competing in our swimming events fun? As we dove a little deeper into 2 Timothy 2, we saw some amazing examples: the good soldier, the athlete, and the farmer. We discovered that to be a true champion for God, we need to give God first place in our lives, please Him, obey His commands, suffer hardship, and endure to the end. Then we will be sure to receive the prize. And we saw that we are saved by grace in Christ Jesus, but our deeds show whether we are true believers in Jesus.

WHAT will we uncover as we continue in 2 Timothy 2? Let's head to the gym and find out. We need to get ready for our gymnastic events.

DAY ONE

HIT THE MAT!

"Good work, Molly, that was a great front walkover." Coach Neighbors patted Molly on the back as she finished her floor exercise. "Katie, you're up next." Katie took a deep breath as the music started and she began her routine.

"Fantastic, girls, I think we're ready for tomorrow. Why don't you clean up—we going to meet the boys at Hardaway Hall to work on 2 Timothy."

Today, let's put ourselves back in the context of 2 Timothy 2. We want to see what characteristics we can discover in 2 Timothy 2:1-13 that describe a faithful follower of Jesus. Don't forget to talk to God!

Turn to page 161 and read 2 Timothy 2:1-13. The characteristics of a true believer listed below are from these verses. Draw a line from the first part of the statement on the left to the statement that it matches on the right.

Entrust the gospel	service
Suffer	the rules
Active	to faithful men
Does not entangle himself	prize
Pleases the one who	hardship
Competes according to	all things
Wins the	Christ
Endures	enlisted him
Died with	we will reign with Him
If we endure	in affairs of everyday life

Now, do you see any characteristics in these verses that describe an unbeliever? Look at 2 Timothy 2:12. WHAT part of this true statement would describe an unbeliever?

_____

Great work! Let's discover our new memory verse. Look at

the exercise mat in the gym on the next page. Coach Neighbors has taped some letters in squares on our mat to help us exercise our mind and discover our new memory verse.

Look at the pair of letters and numbers under each blank. Then go to the exercise mat and find the letter such as A on the right side of the mat, and then go up until you find the number that goes with the A such as 4. Find the letter in the square that goes with A4 and fill it in on the blank. Do the same thing for each blank until you have discovered your verse for the week.

___ ____ ___

E2 D1 D3 D2 A3 A5 A5 D2 B2 D1 B1

_____ _____ ___

A2 D1 E3 C4 C3 D2 E3 A3 A3 E3 E5 C4 E5 B3 E2 D5

_____ _____'

A4 E3 B2 E5 E3 A5 B2 B4 A1 C3 C4 A5 D1 E3 E5 E2 A5 E5 E5

_____, ____ ___ _____,

D2 B3 B4 C4 C3 A3 D1 C1 A5 B3 E2 D5 A4 A5 B3 C2 A5

____ _____ ___ ____

D3 B4 C4 C3 C4 C3 D1 E5 A5 D3 C3 D1 C2 B3 A3 A3

__ ___ ____ ____ _

D1 E2 C4 C3 A5 A3 D1 B2 D5 D3 B4 C4 C3 B3

____ _____.

A4 E3 B2 A5 C3 A5 B3 B2 C4

2 Timothy 2: _____

All right! Don't forget to write your verse out and practice saying it out loud three times today!

DAY TWO
FLIP FOR GOD!

"Man, that was awesome!" Max turned to Matthew. "Did you see those handsprings and backflips? I never knew Katie could flip like that!"

"Look, Max, here comes her score." Josh punched Max. "Man, she got three 9s! Katie got three 9s! All right! Go Team USA!"

Wes looked at Max. "Molly's up next."

"Here she comes," Josh said, "and there she goes." All the guys laughed at Josh's craziness as Molly started her floor exercise. "Man," Josh exclaimed. "I hope we do as well as the girls are. Look—here comes Molly's score…she got a 9, another 9, and an 8.8. Katie got the gold, and Molly got the silver. Way to go, girls!"

All right! How did you like competing in the floor exercise? Even though it is a lot of hard work, we are having so much fun!

Let's head back to 2 Timothy 2. Don't forget to talk to God, our heavenly Coach!

Turn to page 162. Read 2 Timothy 2:14-21 and mark the key words listed below (and any synonyms).

remind (circle in blue)

gospel (and synonyms for the gospel: *these things* [verse 14], *word of truth* [verse 15], *the truth* [verse18]) (draw a red megaphone like this: ⊂◯ and color it green.)

God (Father, Lord) (draw a purple triangle and color it yellow)

ashamed (turned away) (draw a brown arch over it like this: ⌒)

Don't forget to mark your pronouns!

All right! Now, let's ask the 5 W's and an H.

2 Timothy 2:14 WHAT is Paul's instruction to Timothy?

_____

Turn to page 162 and draw a green box around this instruction. WHO is the *them*? Do you know? Look back at 2 Timothy 2:2.

Timothy is to entrust these things to WHOM?

_____

2 Timothy 2:14 WHAT does Paul tell Timothy to charge them? WHAT are they not to do?

_____

WHY? _____

_____

2 Timothy 2:15 WHAT is Paul's instruction?

_____

To be diligent is to make an effort, to be careful in your work. Turn to page 162 and draw a green box around this instruction.

2 Timothy 2:15 WHAT are you to be like?

_____

WHY doesn't the workman have to be ashamed?

_____

We have to be careful how we handle God's Word. God's Word is just that—it is God's Word. It is not to be changed or twisted or made to say what you want it to say. It is the truth! It shows us how to live. And only if you handle it that way will you be approved by God. The Greek word for *approved* is *dokimos*, which is pronounced like this: *dok-ee-mos. Dokimos* means to be put to the test and to pass the test.

Are you careful with God's Word? Do you study it so you make sure you know WHAT it says? Or do you just listen to WHAT others teach and believe WHAT they say? Write out WHAT you do.

_____

By the way, you're studying it for yourself right now! Way to go—we are so proud of you!

2 Timothy 2:16 WHAT is Paul's instruction?

_____

WHY? _____

Turn to page 162 and draw a green box around this instruction.

2 Timothy 2:17 WHAT do we see about this kind of talking? _____

2 Timothy 2:17-18 WHO are these men who talk like this? _____

2 Timothy 2:18 WHAT are they saying that is not true?

_____

If what they are teaching is not true, are they false teachers? _____

Are they accurately handling God's Word? _____

2 Timothy 2:19 WHAT do we see about God's foundation? _____

2 Timothy 2:19 WHAT is this seal?

The _____ _____ those who are

_____, and, _____ who _____

the _____ of the _____ is to _____

from _____.

Awesome! God knows those who are really His! You may fool some people into thinking you are a believer but you can't fool God!

2 Timothy 2:19 WHAT is the instruction to the one who names the name of the Lord?

_____

Turn to page 162 and draw a green box around this instruction.

All right! Way to go! Today as we looked at Paul's instructions to Timothy, we saw that Timothy was to remind faithful men about the gospel and to charge them not to wrangle, to argue with words that will hurt those who are listening. They were to be diligent, to be careful how they handled God's Word, to make sure they were teaching the truth, and to avoid worldly and empty chatter. Do you ever hear people who are always arguing about the Bible being untrue? That is worldly and empty chatter.

We also saw that God knows those who are really His! And if we are His, we are to abstain from wickedness! Remember, the things we believe and the things we do show whether we are true believers in Jesus Christ.

Are you doing that? Do you stay away from things you know are wrong? Name something wrong that you stay away from.

_____

Look up and read 1 Corinthians 9:26-27.

WHAT are we to do to our body?

_____

WHY? _____

Isn't that cool? We are to discipline our body in such a way that we won't be disqualified. The word *disqualified* in this verse is *dokimos*, the same Greek word translated "approved" in 2 Timothy 2:15. We are to compete in such a way that when we are tested we will pass the test!

Tomorrow we will find out more about those who belong to

God and those who don't. Don't forget to practice your memory verse as you head back to the gym for more fun!

DAY THREE
STICK IT!

Molly, Katie, Morgan, and Bethany sat in the stands as the boys got ready for their turn in the floor exercise. "How do you think the boys will do?" Morgan asked Molly. "They have been practicing really hard...I think they will do well."

"There goes Wes," Morgan said as Wes flipped across the mat.

The girls stood up and cheered as the boys finished. "Way to go, guys; you did great!" Coach Neighbors congratulated Wes on his bronze medal. "Way to go, buddy! That was some hard work! All you guys did well. Let's go meet the girls."

Let's head back to 2 Timothy 2. Pray and ask God to help you. Turn to page 162 and read 2 Timothy 2:20-21.

Let's ask the 5 W's and an H to solve the crossword puzzle on the next page.

2 Timothy 2:20 WHERE are these vessels?

1. (Down) In a _____ 2. (Across) _____

This large house that Paul is talking about is the church.

2 Timothy 2:20 WHAT do we see about these vessels?

Some are vessels to 3. (Across) _____ and some to 4. (Down) _____.

2 Timothy 2:21 HOW are we to be vessels of honor?

5. (Down) If anyone _____ himself from these things

Look up and read 1 Corinthians 15:33 to see HOW we can cleanse ourselves and be vessels of honor.

1 Corinthians 15:33 WHAT does bad company do?

6. (Across) _____ good 7. (Across) _____

So to be vessels of honor, we need to cleanse ourselves by separating from vessels of dishonor. We need to be careful about the company we keep, whom we hang out with. Look up and read 2 Thessalonians 3:6.

2 Thessalonians 3:6 WHOM are we to keep away from?

Every brother who leads an 8. (Across) _____

9. (Down) _____

2 Timothy 2:21 If we are vessels of honor, WHAT will we be?

10. (Across) _____, 11. (Down) _____

to the 12. (Down)_____, 13. (Down)_____

for every 14. (Across) _____ 15. (Down)

_____

Wow! Which do you want to be—a vessel of honor that is sanctified, set apart, and useful to God for every good work, or a vessel of dishonor?

_____

Which of these vessels represents believers?

_____

Which of these vessels represents unbelievers?

_____

Today we have seen two different types of vessels in the church—those that are of gold and silver and are for honor, and those that are wood and earthenware for dishonor.

To be a vessel of honor that God can use, we have to cleanse ourselves from these things, these vessels of dishonor. Remember, bad company corrupts good morals. Second Corinthians 6:14 says, "Do not be bound together with unbelievers; for what partnership have righteousness and lawlessness, or what fellowship has light with darkness?"

In order to be used by God, we have to be set apart—different from the world we live in. Do you hang out with kids who care nothing about God? _____ Watch out!

WHAT kind of kids do you hang out with? Kids who love God and do what God says is right or kids who go in the opposite direction, who do what pleases them, and who participate in the things that God says are sin?

_____

WHAT are your best friends like? Put a checkmark next to the statements that apply to them.

- Your best friends obey their parents. _____

- Your best friends don't raise their voices and talk ugly to their parents. They respect their parents. _____

- Your best friends lie to their parents. _____

- Your best friends go to movies they shouldn't see. _____

- Your best friends use bad words. _____

Vessels of honor have to separate themselves from vessels of dishonor, from those who are walking in the opposite direction from God and who are living an ungodly lifestyle. We saw that we are to keep away from a brother who lives an unruly life. If we are set apart and allowing God to work in our hearts and our lives, then we will be prepared to do whatever God asks us to do.

WHAT else can you learn about being a vessel of honor that God can use? You'll find out tomorrow as you continue to look at 2 Timothy 2. Here's a hint: Practice your memory verse.

DAY FOUR
SOMERSAULT INTO ACTION

"Hey, Max," Molly looked around. "Where's Sam?" Max turned around and looked for Sam.

"Uh-oh, we're in trouble now." Max moaned. "Let's spread out to look for him. You know how he loves to get into mischief. Sam, Sam, where are you, boy?" Max whistled as he called for Sam.

Coach Neighbors walked up to Max. "Hey, Max, don't worry about Sam. One of the coaches saw him wandering around and took him for a little special training. You know how bad he's wanted to get out on the exercise mat. Well, Coach Allen decided to give him a chance to do his own floor exercise. Why don't you and the team start your training on 2 Timothy."

Let's head back to 2 Timothy 2. Don't forget to talk to God.

Turn to page 163. Read 2 Timothy 2:22-26 and mark the key words listed below (and their synonyms).

gospel (the truth) (draw a red megaphone like this: ⊲◯ and color it green)

God (Father, Lord) (draw a purple triangle and color it yellow)

Yesterday as we looked at the vessels in a large house (the church), we saw a contrast. We saw some vessels of honor and some vessels of dishonor. We saw that to be a vessel of honor we are to cleanse ourselves, and we learned that one way we can do that is to watch the company we keep. WHAT else can we do to be set apart and useful to the Master for every good work?

Two instructions in 2 Timothy 2:22 show us how to become vessels of honor. WHAT is the first instruction? WHAT are you to do?

F __ __ __ from _____ _____.

Turn to page 163 and draw a green box around this instruction.

Wow! Have you ever turned on your computer and seen something you shouldn't see? When you are tempted, you are to flee, to run away from youthful lusts. Lusts are wrong desires and impulses that lead to sin. In order to be a vessel of honor, you need to get away from anything—a thought, an action, or even people—that will lead you to sin.

WHAT are you going to do the next time you are tempted to say a bad word, look at something on the Internet you know is wrong, or hang out with the wrong crowd? _____

2 Timothy 2:22 WHAT are you to do after you flee? WHAT is the second instruction?

P __ __ __ __ __ _____, _____,

_____, and _____

Turn to page 163 and draw a green box around this instruction.

HOW do you pursue righteousness? HOW do you know the right thing to do? WHAT do you need to do every day so you can know God and do what He says is right?

_____.

HOW do you pursue faith? Faith is taking God at His Word. Faith is believing Him and showing it by the way you act. Do you listen and pay attention to His Word?_____

WHAT do you do that shows you believe God?

_____

Have you accepted Jesus Christ as your Savior? Have you trusted God with your life? _____

_____

HOW can you pursue love? Look up and read Mark 12:30-31.

Mark 12:30 WHAT are you to do?

_____

_____

Mark 12:31 WHOM else are you to love?

_____

Wow! We are to love others and even put them before ourselves. And that doesn't just mean the people we like. We are to love everyone—even our enemies (Matthew 5:44).

Write out a way you are going to love your neighbor.

_____

HOW will you pursue peace? Look at 2 Timothy 2:24. WHAT must the Lord's bond-servant not be?

Q _ _ _ _ _ _ _ _ _ _

One way you can pursue peace is to try to get along with others.

WHOM do you fuss and argue with—your parents, your brothers or sisters, kids at school, your teacher…?

_____

WHAT can you do to get along with others?

_____

Now, look back at 2 Timothy 2:22. WHOM are we to pursue these things with?

Those who _____

_____

Once again you see the importance of hanging out with the right kids. You need to be friends with kids who pursue God, kids who have a pure heart.

WHOM do you hang out with—kids who follow God,

or kids who are cool and popular? _____

_____

If you don't have a friend who follows God, ask God to help you find one whom you can get to know and hang out with.

2 Timothy 2:23 WHAT is Paul's instruction?

_____

WHY? WHAT do they produce? _____

Turn to page 163 and draw a green box around this instruction.

2 Timothy 2:24-25 WHAT do we learn about the Lord's bond-servant?

_____

_____

_____

Do you know what a bond-servant is? A bond-servant is a person who has chosen to be a slave after he has been offered his freedom. To be a bond-servant is to willingly become a slave for life. To be God's bond-servant is to totally surrender your life to serve God and Jesus.

Have you considered telling the Lord you want to be His bond-servant? Have you surrendered your life and your way for God's way? _____

Do you have the qualities of a bond-servant listed in 2 Timothy 2:24-25? Write out the qualities that you see in your life.

_____

_____

WHAT qualities do you need to ask God to help you work on?

_____

2 Timothy 2:25 WHY are we to have these qualities in our lives? WHAT are we to do with gentleness?

_____

Did you get it? We are not to quarrel with those who are opposing God. We are to be kind and gentle with them when we correct what they are doing wrong. We are to be able to teach them, to show them what they are doing or believing is wrong. And we are also to be patient if they lash out or hurt us.

We are to show people the truth, but we are to do it with the character of Jesus, not getting mad and responding in anger. We are to show them that we are different and that we belong to Jesus by the way we act and treat them. And WHAT may happen?

2 Timothy 2:25 WHAT may God grant these vessels of dishonor?

_____

2 Timothy 2:26 WHOM are they held captive by?

_____

2 Timothy 2:26 WHAT may happen to them?

_____

Wow! When you act like Jesus by correcting others with gentleness and showing them the truth, God may allow them to come to their senses so that they repent and turn to the truth. Isn't that awesome! What a way for God to use you!

Now, don't forget to practice your memory verse.

DAY FIVE
SHOWTIME!

Are you ready to see Sam in action?   Look, here he comes! Look at those ribbons he is carrying in his mouth. He is going to do some rhythmic gymnastics. WOW! Did you see that? Sam did a flip! There he goes, jumping through a ring this time. Amazing! Will Sam get a medal? The crowd is going crazy. Uh-oh, there he goes. He sees Max. All right! Way to go, Sam!

Wasn't that fun watching Sam? He was feeling a little left out, but not anymore. Now he has his own medal. Give Sam a doggie treat and let's head back to 2 Timothy 2.

Have you noticed that Paul shows Timothy how to distinguish between the believers and the unbelievers? Today we want to look back at 2 Timothy 2:14-26 and find the characteristics that describe believers and unbelievers, just as we did on day one for 2 Timothy 2:1-13.

Don't forget to pray and ask God to help you see what describes a true believer and what describes an unbeliever.

Turn to page 162 and read 2 Timothy 2:14-26. As you read each verse, ask yourself WHOM this describes?

> 2 Timothy 2:14 WHO is the *them* in this verse? Remember, we saw that the *them* were the faithful men in 2 Timothy 2:2. So WHO are the faithful men—believers or unbelievers?

_____

On the following chart, under Characteristics of a Believer, write what this verse tells us about a believer. Then fill in the rest of the chart, writing the characteristics from each verse that describe a believer.

Characteristics of a Believer

2 Timothy 2:14 A believer is not to _____

about _____.

2 Timothy 2:15 Is d __ __ __ __ __ __ __. _____

himself to God as a _____ who does not need

to be _____, _____ handling

the _____ of _____.

2 Timothy 2:16 Avoids _____ and _____

_____.

2 Timothy 2:19 Abstains from _____.

2 Timothy 2:20 A vessel of _____.

2 Timothy 2:21 _____ himself. He is

s __ __ __ __ __ __ __ __ __, _____ to the

_____, _____ for every _____

_____.

2 Timothy 2:22 _____ from youthful _____

and pursues _____, _____,

_____, and _____, with those who call on

the Lord from a _____ heart.

2 Timothy 2:23 Refuses _____ and

_____ speculations.

2 Timothy 2:24 The Lord's _____-_____,

not _____, _____to all, able to

_____, _____ when wronged.

2 Timothy 2:25 Corrects with _____

those who are in _____.

Now look back at these same verses and list any characteristics in the chart below that describe an unbeliever.

Characteristics of an Unbeliever

2 Timothy 2:17 Their _____ spreads like

_____.

2 Timothy 2:18 They have gone astray from the

_____ and upset the _____ of some.

2 Timothy 2:20 Vessels of _____.

2 Timothy 2:25 In o __ __ __ __ __ __ __ __ __ to God.

2 Timothy 2:26 In the snare of the _____,
held _____ by him to do his _____.

Wow, which characteristics do you have?

_____

_____

Think about what you have learned. Now say your memory verse to a grown-up to remind you of what you are to do to be a vessel of honor! We are so proud of you!

5

CONTINUE IN THE THINGS YOU HAVE LEARNED

2 TIMOTHY 3

Are you ready for another exciting week in our summer games?

Last week as we looked at Paul's instructions to Timothy, we saw that Timothy was to remind faithful men about the gospel and to charge them to not wrangle about words. They were to be diligent and to accurately handle God's Word, making sure they were teaching the truth!

We also saw that the church includes vessels of honor that are set apart and useful to God, and vessels of dishonor. And that as the Lord's bond-servants, we are to correct those who are in opposition so that God may lead them to repent and turn to the truth! What a way to be a champion for God!

WHAT we will learn this week? Let's head to the archery field and find out.

DAY ONE

BRACING THE BOW

"Okay, guys, brace the bow," Coach Neighbors told Team USA

as they got out their bows on the field. "Now, stand, nock (set the arrow in the bowstring), and draw. Looking good. Release and follow through. All right, guys, that was great! Walk over to your target and see how you did. That was a great archery practice.

"Now pull out your books, and let's get some Bible training in. Bethany, why don't you pray for us."

Let's turn to page 163. Read 2 Timothy 3 and mark the key words listed below (and their synonyms).

God (Father) (draw a purple triangle and color it yellow)

suffering (persecutions, persecuted) (draw a red squiggly line like this: ⟿)

Christ Jesus (draw a purple cross and color it yellow)

Look in verses 10, 11, and 15 for any exhortations that Paul gives Timothy and draw a pink cloud around the words of encouragement.

Verses 1,5, and 14 contain three instructions to Timothy. Draw a green box around each instruction.

Don't forget to mark anything that tells you WHERE by double underlining the WHERE in green. Mark anything that tells you WHEN by drawing a green clock 🕐 or green circle like this: ◯ .

Fantastic! Let's discover our memory verse. Look at the arrows in the target on the next page. Each arrow has a number on the feather. Look at the number and find the matching blank below. Write the word written on each arrow on the correct blank to solve this week's verse. Then turn to 2 Timothy 3 and find the reference for this verse.

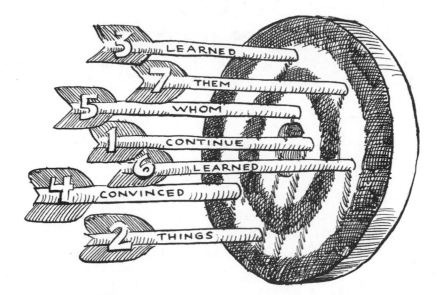

You, however, _____ in the _____ you have
                         1   2

_____ and become _____ of,
          3   4

knowing from _____ you have _____
                      5   6

_____.   2 Timothy 3: _____
       7

Now write it out and practice saying it three times in a row today. Stand, nock, draw, release, and follow through! Way to hit the target!

DAY TWO

AIMING FOR THE TARGET

"Max, you're up." Coach Neighbors stood beside Max, giving him his last-minute instructions. "Remember, when your drawing hand reaches your anchor point, hold it tight against your face for a few seconds to steady your aim. Keep your eyes on the bull's-eye.

"Next, tighten your back and shoulder muscles, open the fingers of your drawing hand, and release."

"You can do it, Max," cheered the rest of Team USA while Sam barked his agreement.

All right! Did you see that? Max got a 5, a 7, an 8, another 8, and a bull's-eye. Way to go, Max! Team USA is on its way to another medal!

Now, let's head back to our Bible training and give our best to God. Don't forget to pray. Turn to page 163 and read 2 Timothy 3:1-5.

Let's ask the 5 W's and an H.

2 Timothy 3:1 WHAT is Paul's instruction?

R _ _ _ _ _ _   t _ _ _

Did you remember to put a green box around this instruction?

2 Timothy 3:1 WHEN is this going to happen?

_____

Did you know that we are living in the last days right now? The last days started when Jesus began His ministry on earth and will end when He comes back again the second time. We are living in the last days!

2 Timothy 3:1 WHAT do we need to realize? WHAT is going to happen in the last days?

_____

That means things will continue to get worse and worse and worse, and yet the world will think things will get better and better.

Did you know that the New Testament, where the book of 2 Timothy is found, was originally written in Koine Greek? The Greek word for the word *men* in verse 2 is *anthrôpos*. It is pronounced like this: *anth-ro-pos*. This word means a human being, people, or mankind. So when you read verse 2, the word for *men* actually refers to all people, not just men.

2 Timothy 3:2-5 HOW are these men (people) described?

List the characteristics of these men. _____

_____

_____

_____

_____

_____

Are these characteristics of believers or unbelievers?

_____

Let's look at a few of these characteristics and think about what they mean.

WHAT does it mean to be a lover of self?

Do you remember what we saw last week in Mark 12:30-31 as we looked at pursuing love? We saw that we are to love God with all our heart, with all our soul, with all our mind, and with all our strength. And we are to love others as ourselves. A lover of self puts the focus on himself. It's all about *me*, not loving God or our neighbors. Are you a lover of self?

Do you love yourself more than others? __ Yes __ No

Do you have to be first and have your way? __ Yes __ No

Do you put yourself ahead of others? __ Yes __ No

Look up and read Philippians 2:3-8.

Philippians 2:3 HOW are we to regard others?

_____

Philippians 2:6 WHO was Jesus? Jesus was G __ __!

Philippians 2:7 WHAT did Jesus do?

He _____ Himself, taking on the form of a

_____-_____ .

Philippians 2:8 WHAT else did He do?

He _____ Himself by becoming _____
to the point of death.

We are to be like Jesus. Even though Jesus was God, He took on the form of a bond-servant, became a man, obeyed God, and gave up His life for us! *Amazing!* We are to humble ourselves by putting others first. We are not to love ourselves more than others. We are to give ourselves for others just as Jesus gave Himself for us!

Let's look at some other characteristics.

HOW important is money to you?

Matthew 6:24 tells us that we cannot serve two masters. We cannot serve God and wealth. HOW about you?

Do you covet (long with envy for) everything your friends have? _____ Yes _____ No

Are you greedy? Do you want more and more? Do you have to have the newest and the latest things? _____ Yes _____ No

Are you boastful?

Do you brag about how great you are or the things that you have, or do you realize that everything that you are and that you have comes from God? Write out what you do.

_____

Are you disobedient to your parents?

Look up and read Ephesians 6:1-3.

Ephesians 6:1-2 WHAT are children to do?

_____

Ephesians 6:3 WHAT is the promise if you obey and honor your parents? _____

_____

Are you ungrateful?

Do you bug your parents to buy things? Are you unsatisfied with the things that you have? ___ Yes ___ No

Are you thankful for the people who love you and the things God has blessed you with? ___ Yes ___ No

Look up and read 1 Thessalonians 5:18.

WHAT is God's will for you?

_____

Let's look at one more of these characteristics.

Do you hold to a form of godliness?

People who hold to a form of godliness are people who pretend to be Christians, but they are not really believers. They do religious things and act like Christians on the outside, but there isn't a change on the inside. They have not turned their lives over to Jesus. So HOW about you? Do you go to church and say all the right things but then do what you want to do instead of what pleases God? For example…

Do you lie to your parents? ___ Yes ___ No

Do you make fun of other kids? ___ Yes ___ No

Do you look at bad stuff on the Internet? ___ Yes ___ No

Wow! Do you see any of these descriptions in your life? If you do see any of these things in your life, WHAT do you do? Look up and read 1 John 1:9.

WHAT are we to do?

_____

WHAT will God do?

_____

_____

Isn't that awesome? God loves you so much that He forgives you when you fail. But don't think these things don't matter. They do. It's easy to act like everybody else. People who are vessels of dishonor want us to act just like them. But we are to act like Jesus, not like everybody else. Ask God for His help so the world can see Jesus living in you!

And if you see that you are only pretending to be a Christian, tell a grown-up that you really want to know Jesus and have a relationship with Him, and he or she will help you give your life to Jesus.

> Look back at 2 Timothy 3:5 WHAT was Paul's instruction?
>
> _____
>
> WHAT are we to do about the people we just described?
>
> _____

Remember what we learned. Bad company corrupts good morals. To be vessels of honor that God can use, we need to stay away from people like these!

All right! You have hit the target again! Don't forget to practice your memory verse!

DAY THREE
HOLD AND RELEASE

Way to go! That was an awesome shot. What a steady arm and quick release. Team USA is so excited about those two bull's-eyes. You helped Team USA bring home another gold medal!

All right! Let's head back to 2 Timothy 3. Turn to page 163 and read 2 Timothy 3:6-9. Let's ask the 5 W's and an H to solve the crossword puzzle on the next page.

2 Timothy 3:6 WHAT do we see about these men?

1. (Down) They _____ 2. (Across) _____ women.

2 Timothy 3:6 WHAT do you learn about these weak women?

They are weighed down with 3. (Across) _____

and led on by various 4. (Across) _____.

These are women (or girls) who don't behave with their bodies and keep them pure.

2 Timothy 3:7 WHAT do we learn about these men?

They are always 5. (Across) _____ and never able to come to the knowledge of the 6. (Down) _____.

2 Timothy 3:8 WHAT do these men do?

7. (Down) They _____ the truth.

2 Timothy 3:8 WHAT are these men like?

They are men of 8. (Down) _____ 9. (Down) _____, 10. (Across) _____ in regard to the 11. (Across) _____.

2 Timothy 3:9 WHAT do we see about these men?

They will not make further 12. (Down) _____; for their 13. (Down) _____ will be 14. (Across) _____ to all.

Are you going to listen to false teachers, those who oppose truth?

2 Timothy 3:5 WHAT does Paul tell you to do?

_____ such _____ as these.

Great work! We are to stay away from these false teachers. And we see that even though these men are opposing truth, they will not make further progress. Their false teaching will be exposed!

Hit the target one more time by practicing your memory verse!

DAY FOUR
RACING UPHILL

That was a great archery competition! Our next event is biking.

Put on those bike helmets and fill up those water bottles. Then head to 2 Timothy 3 and prepare yourself for the race ahead. Don't forget to ask God for His help.

Turn to page 164 and read 2 Timothy 3:10-13. Ask the 5 W's and an H.

2 Timothy 3:10-11 WHAT did Timothy do?

_____

_____

_____

WHAT is Paul doing in these two verses? Paul is encouraging Timothy. Paul reminds Timothy of how Timothy has followed Paul's example. Did you put a pink cloud around this encouragement on your Observation Worksheet?

2 Timothy 3:11 WHAT happened to Paul at Antioch,

Iconium, and Lystra? _____

Look up and read 2 Corinthians 11:24-27. HOW was Paul persecuted?

He received _____-_____ _____ from the Jews five times.

He was _____ with _____ three times.

He was _____ once.

He was _____ three times.

He spent a _____ and a _____ in the

_____.

He has been in danger from _____,

_____, his _____

from the _____, in the _____, in the

_____, on the _____, and among

_____ _____.

He has been in _____ and _____,

through many _____ _____, in

_____ and _____, often without

_____, and in _____ and exposure.

Draw a picture of one of Paul's persecutions in the box below

Go back to 2 Timothy 3:11 WHAT do we see about Paul?

He e __ __ __ __ __ __ !

2 Timothy 3:11 WHAT did the Lord do?

_____

Wow! WHAT an *awesome* God!

2 Timothy 3:12 WHAT will happen to those who desire to live godly in Christ Jesus?

_____

Are you surprised? A lot of people think that when they become Christians everything will be good all the time, and bad things won't happen to them. But that's not true. The Bible never says that. Instead, the Bible tells us we will be persecuted.

Look back at 2 Timothy 3:13 WHAT do you learn about

evil men and imposters? _____

_____

Way to go! Today you have seen how Timothy followed Paul's example, and you got a close-up look at some of Paul's persecutions, how he endured, and how God rescued him! You also saw that everyone who wants to live a godly life will be persecuted.

And you saw that evil men not only are deceived themselves but also deceive other people. Remember to follow Paul's example and avoid these people! All right! Hop on those bikes and get ready to race. Don't forget to practice your memory verse!

DAY FIVE

BREAKAWAY

What a bike race! You have pulled out of the pack and are now in the breakaway group. Keep on pedaling. You are doing great. One more turn and you should be headed downhill. Don't give up!

Look at Sam. He's cheering you on as he rides on Coach Neighbors's motorcycle behind the racers. You did it! You continued your pace and crossed the finish line for a bronze medal. Way to hang in there and win another medal!

Now let's find out how we can continue in the things we have learned to earn a medal as God's champion. Ask God for His help.

Then turn to page 164 and read 2 Timothy 3:14-17. Ask the 5 W's and an H.

2 Timothy 3:14 WHAT was Timothy to do?

_____

Did you remember to put a green box around this instruction?

Look back at 2 Timothy 1:5 WHO in Timothy's family had a sincere faith? WHO taught Timothy?

_____

2 Timothy 3:15 WHAT did Timothy learn?

_____

2 Timothy 3:15 WHEN did he learn the sacred writings?

_____

Did you put a pink cloud around this encouragement from Paul?

2 Timothy 3:15 WHAT are the sacred writings able to give you?

_____

2 Timothy 3:15 WHAT does wisdom lead to?

_____

2 Timothy 3:15 HOW do you receive salvation?

_____

Isn't that awesome! Timothy was taught God's Word as a child. Paul is telling Timothy to continue in what he knows, the sacred writings, God's Word.

God's Word will help you recognize false teaching, it will get you through suffering and persecution, and it will show you how you are to live so you can please God! Remember, you have to know God's Word before you can pass it on to others. And just think—you are becoming a "Timothy" or a "Timeothea" (if you are a girl). You are learning God's Word right now while you are young!

WHAT else can we learn about the Word?

2 Timothy 3:16 WHAT do we see about all Scipture?

It is _____ by God.

The Greek word for *inspired* is *theopneustos*. It is pronounced like this: *theh-op-nyoó-stos*. *Theos* means God, and *pneo* means to breathe. So the word *inspired* (*theopneustos*) means the Scripture is "God-breathed." This is the only place in the whole New Testament that this word is used. Look up and read 2 Peter 1:20-21.

HOW did we get the Scripture? HOW did men know

what to write? Men _____ by the _____

_____ spoke from _____.

Isn't that awesome? We know we can trust what the Bible tells us because it comes directly from God.

2 Timothy 3:16 WHAT are the four things that the Scripture is profitable for?

1. _____

2. _____

3. _____

4. _____

The Bible doesn't contain God's words; it *is* the Word of God. It is "God-breathed" and is good for teaching (so we can know the truth), for reproof (so we can know when we are doing something wrong), for correction (so we can correct what we have done wrong and know how to get it right), and for training in righteousness (so we can live right and have a right relationship with God).

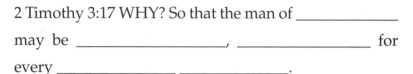

2 Timothy 3:17 WHY? So that the man of _____

may be _____, _____ for

every _____ _____.

That means we will be completely qualified so that we can do the work God has for us. We can live the way God wants us to live! Nothing is more important than knowing God's Word! Now ask yourself:

- Do you believe WHAT the Bible says? ____ Yes ____ No
- Will you choose to believe what the Bible says over what man says? ____ Yes ____ No
- Will you allow God's Word to show you where you are wrong? ____ Yes ____ No
- Are you willing to be corrected? Will you change what's wrong to what's right even if means changing what you believe? ____ Yes ____ No
- Are you willing to be trained in righteousness so God can use you for every good work? ____ Yes ____ No

What an awesome week! Are you willing to continue in the things that you know? WHO did you learn the sacred writings from?

_____

Why don't you tell that person thank you for teaching you God's Word. Now say your verse out loud to a grown-up so you can continue in the things you have learned and become God's champion!

6

PREACH THE GOSPEL

2 TIMOTHY 4

Wow! Can you believe that this is our last week at our summer sports camp? We have learned so much! Last week as we hit our target and raced on our bikes, we saw that we are living in the last days. And we saw how to spot some ungodly men and silly women who oppose the truth and deceive others.

We also saw how Paul was persecuted, how he endured, and how God rescued him. And we saw the importance of Scripture. The Bible doesn't contain God's words; it is the Word of God. It will teach us what is right and what is wrong, and show us how to do what God says is right! It will equip us to do God's work! *Awesome!* What will we discover as we read the final pages of Paul's letter? Let's find out.

DAY ONE

PRACTICE DRILLS

"All right!" Coach Neighbors gathered Team USA together. "Let's get to work on our Bible training. Then we need to head to the soccer field and practice for tomorrow's game. Is everybody ready to find out how Paul ends his letter?"

"We sure are!" shouted Team USA.

"Great! Max, why don't you ask God to help us in our training so we can serve Him!"

Great! Now that we've asked for God's help, let's turn to page 164. Read 2 Timothy 4 and mark the key words listed below and any synonyms.

God (draw a purple triangle and color it yellow)

Christ Jesus (Lord, Judge) (draw a purple cross and color it yellow)

gospel (and synonyms for the gospel: *the word* [verse 2], *sound doctrine* [verse 3], *the truth* [verse 4], *proclamation* [verse 17]) (draw a red megaphone like this:◁◯ and color it green)

turn away (turn aside) (draw a brown arch over it like this: ⌒)

Look for any instructions to Timothy and draw a green box around each instruction.

Don't forget to mark your pronouns! And don't forget to double underline the WHERE in green and anything that tells you WHEN with a green clock 🕐 or green circle ◯ .

Fantastic! Now, grab your soccer ball and work on your skills as you find the correct path on the soccer field maze. Figure out how to score a goal and solve this week's memory verse. Then fill in the blanks with the correct words on the lines underneath the soccer field.

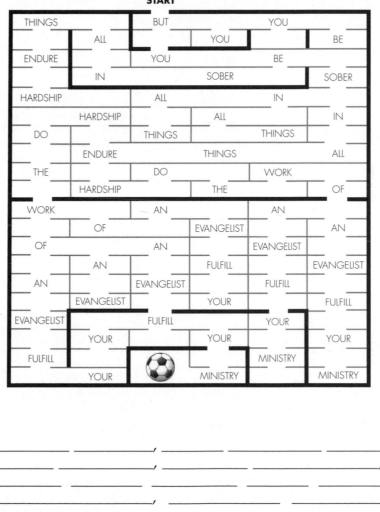

START

THINGS · BUT · YOU · BE
ALL · YOU · BE
ENDURE · YOU · BE · SOBER
IN · SOBER · SOBER
HARDSHIP · ALL · IN
HARDSHIP · ALL · IN
DO · THINGS · THINGS
ENDURE · THINGS · ALL
THE · DO · WORK
HARDSHIP · THE · OF
WORK · AN · AN
OF · EVANGELIST · AN
OF · AN · EVANGELIST
AN · FULFILL · EVANGELIST
AN · EVANGELIST · FULFILL
EVANGELIST · YOUR · FULFILL
EVANGELIST · FULFILL · YOUR
YOUR · YOUR · YOUR
FULFILL · MINISTRY
YOUR · MINISTRY · MINISTRY

_____ _____, _____ _____ _____

_____ _____, _____ _____ _____,

____ _____ _____ _____ _____

_____, _____ _____

_____.

2 Timothy 4: _____

Way to score! Don't forget to practice saying your verse out
loud three times today!

DAY TWO

SHOOT!

"Molly, Max is wide open…pass it to Max," Coach Neighbors shouted across the soccer field. "Go, Max…way to take it down field. You've got it! Great pass. Morgan, take the shot! All right! Way to go, Team USA! Great shot, Morgan. Great assist, Max."

There goes the whistle, and it's another win for Team USA. Coach Neighbors hugged the kids as they ran off the field. "Way to play as a team instead of putting yourself first. Great pass, Molly. Max, I am so proud of the way you passed to Morgan instead of taking the shot. Way to go, Team! Let's hit the showers and get back to 2 Timothy."

What a great game! Ask God to help you be a good team player as a member of His team. Then turn to page 164 and read 2 Timothy 4:1-5.

Let's ask the 5 W's and an H to find out what Paul's final words are to Timothy as he wraps up his letter.

2 Timothy 4:1 WHAT is Paul doing? WHAT does he say to Timothy?

I _____ _____ you

2 Timothy 4:1 In WHOSE presence does Paul make this charge?

_____

Do you see the seriousness of this charge? Paul wanted Timothy to know how important his final words are.

2 Timothy 4:1 WHAT do we learn about Jesus in this verse?

He is to _____ the _____ and the

_____ by His _____

and His _____.

Wow! When Jesus comes back, He is going to judge the living and the dead! Did you know that Christians will be judged? Second Corinthians 5:10 tells us we will all appear before the judgment seat of Christ for the things we have done, whether good or bad. We are saved by God's grace and will live with Jesus forever, but we are rewarded for our deeds.

Charging Timothy in God's presence is like standing before God and Jesus face-to-face. Every person will one day stand before God and Jesus either at the judgment seat of Christ, where Christians are judged (2 Corinthians 5:10); (Revelation 20:4-6), or at the Great White Throne judgment, where unbelievers (the dead) are judged (Revelation 20:11-12).

> 2 Timothy 4:2 WHAT is the charge? WHAT is Timothy to do?

_____

Did you put a green box around this instruction?

WHAT does it mean to preach the word? The Greek word for *preach* is *kêrussô*. It is pronounced like this: *kay-roos-so*. It means to herald or proclaim the divine truth, the gospel.

In Paul's day, the rulers had heralds that made special announcements to the people in loud, clear voices so everyone could hear and heed the message. Timothy is to herald the gospel so the people can hear and heed it.

> 2 Timothy 4:2 WHEN is Timothy to be ready?

_____

That means Timothy is to preach the gospel when it is convenient and when it isn't. Paul always found an opportunity to share the Word whether he was in the temple, in the courts, or on the stormy sea. Paul was telling Timothy to use every opportunity to preach the Word and not to make excuses about it not being a good time or a good place.

Remember, Timothy is living in a time when Christians are being persecuted. It is not an easy time to share the gospel, but Paul charges him in God and Jesus' presence that Timothy is to preach the gospel at all times!

2 Timothy 2:2 HOW is he to preach the word?

He is to _____, _____,

_____, with great _____ and

_____.

To reprove means to tell someone he is doing something wrong. To rebuke is to admonish and warn someone. And you already know that to exhort is to encourage.

Timothy is preach the Word at all times, telling others what they are doing wrong, warning them, and encouraging them. He is to be patient and give them the right teaching. Timothy is to guard the treasure. He needs to make sure others know the truth of the gospel.

2 Timothy 4:3 WHY is it so important to know the truth? WHAT will happen in time?

For a time will come when they _____ _____

_____ _____ _____.

2 Timothy 4:3 WHAT will they want instead of sound (healthy) doctrine (teaching)?

_____

2 Timothy 4:3 WHAT will they accumulate for themselves?

_____

2 Timothy 4:4 WHAT will they turn their ears away from?

_____

2 Timothy 4:4 WHAT will they turn to?

_____

Whoa, do you see how bad these last days are? A time will come when people will no longer want the truth but will want to have their ears tickled. Tickling your ear feels good. Here, it means telling people things that make them feel good but that aren't good for them. That means people will want teachers and preachers who tell them what they want to hear instead of the truth. That way, they can do what they want to do and not have someone correct and admonish them.

HOW does this compare to our world today? Do we have false teachers? _____ Do you know people who don't want to know the truth so they can live any way they want to? _____

WHY is it so important for Timothy to preach the Word in these last days? WHY is it so important for us to know and teach the truth?

_____

_____

2 Timothy 4:5 WHAT does Paul tell Timothy to do?

_____

_____

Did you put a green box around the instructions?

Paul tells Timothy to be watchful, to be serious about his work, to endure hardships, to do the work of an evangelist. An evangelist is someone who shares the gospel. You can be an evangelist by telling kids at school or in your neighborhood about Jesus.

You could take a mission trip to another city in the U.S. or in another country. On your mission trip, you could share the gospel with others as you help build a school or a church. You could teach kids to study the Bible the same way you do. You could tell them how you came to know Jesus, feed the poor, and help those who are sick.

You can share the gospel in lots of ways. Timothy is to fulfill his ministry, to do the work God has for him to do. God has a ministry for each one of us to fulfill. We all have different gifts, and God will use us in many different ways.

WHAT are your gifts? Do you like to teach, sing, draw, play sports, work with your hands, cook, create, write, learn, or help others?

Write out what your gifts are.

_____

God will use some of us to teach and some of us to take care of our homes and raise godly families. Some of us will care for the sick, some will work in a business, some will serve others, some will go on the mission field; and some will know that their mission field is in their own neighborhood or school. What we do doesn't matter as long as we follow God and use our gifts to serve Him. And regardless of what our gifts are, we all have one thing that we are to do, and that's to share the good news about Jesus with others.

How can God use you? _____

_____

Awesome! Now, don't forget to practice your memory verse!

DAY THREE
SLIDE TACKLE

"All right, Wes!" Coach Neighbors patted Wes's back as he came out for a break. "That was a great slide tackle. Way to get the ball back. Come on, Josh, get it to Max. Shoot, Max, shoot!"

Did you see that? Max shot the winning goal for Team USA! We have two more games to play to find out who wins the gold medal. Aren't you excited? Let's head to our team meeting and find out what Paul has to say to Timothy.

Talk to God. Then turn to page 165. Read 2 Timothy 4:6-8 and ask the 5 W's and an H.

2 Timothy 4:6 WHAT do we see about Paul?

_____

Paul uses this description of the Old Testament drink offering being poured out as a sacrifice to show that his life is being poured out. He is giving his life as a sacrifice for Jesus.

2 Timothy 4:6 WHAT is it time for?

_____

Paul knows he is going to die. He is going home to heaven to be with God and Jesus.

2 Timothy 4:7 WHAT does Paul say about himself?

_____

_____

2 Timothy 4:8 WHAT will Paul receive in the future?

_____

2 Timothy 4:8 WHO will award this crown to Paul?

_____

2 Timothy 4:8 WHEN will he receive this crown?

_____

2 Timothy 4:8 Is Paul the only one to receive this crown?

_____

WHO else receives this crown?

_____

Wow! We have seen in Revelation 22:12 that when Jesus comes back, His reward will be with Him. Now we see what one of those rewards is—the crown of righteousness that is given to those who have loved Jesus' appearing.

Last week we drew a picture of Paul's persecutions. Today let's draw a picture in the box below to show Paul's reward for fighting the good fight and finishing the course. Draw a picture of Paul receiving the crown of righteousness from Jesus.

Does the Bible talk about crowns in any other places? WHAT other crowns are there?

Look up and read James 1:12. WHAT is this crown?

_____

HOW do you get it? _____

_____

Look up and read Revelation 2:10. WHAT crown is given? _____

Look up and read 1 Peter 5:4. WHAT crown will be given when the Chief Shepherd (Jesus) appears?

_____

This crown is for the shepherd of the flock. It is a crown that will be given to pastors.

Look up and read 1 Thessalonians 2:19. WHAT is the crown in this verse? The crown of _____.

Wow! Just look at all you have seen today. You have seen that Paul is being poured out as a drink offering. He is giving his life as a sacrifice for Jesus.

Paul is about to die. He will depart from this world to spend eternity with Jesus. As Paul prepares to die, he looks back at his life. Look at what he says about himself: "I have fought the good fight." Like a boxer, he has given his best in the contest. " I have finished the course." Like a runner in a race, he has obeyed the rules, he finished the race, and now will receive a prize. "I have kept the faith." Paul has guarded the treasure that God gave him.

After Paul looks back, he looks ahead to the future at the crown he will receive because he has been faithful. Paul has lived his life for Jesus! He will receive the prize of an imperishable crown (1 Corinthians 9:25).

Amazing! Are you going to live your life so you can receive the prize? Will Jesus reward you with one of these awesome crowns so you can lay it at His feet to thank Him for all He's done for you?

Don't forget to practice your memory verse.

DAY FOUR

DEFEND THE GOAL

"Way to defend the goal, Matthew!" Coach Neighbors called out from the sidelines. "Okay, let's have a good throw-in. Good, good. Dribble that ball. Bethany, take it. Okay, Max, shoot! All right! One more goal for Team USA. You can do it!

"Here it comes. Matthew, be ready; defend the goal. All right! Way to kick it out of there. Take it Molly. Run, Molly, run—take it all the way. Pass—Josh is open. Shoot, Josh! You did it! Three to two! You just defeated Team Greece. Only one more game to a gold medal."

What an incredible day for Team USA. Let's get our minds focused to prepare for tomorrow's deciding game by doing our training in 2 Timothy. Don't forget to pray. Turn to page 165 and read 2 Timothy 4:9-22.

Let's take a look at Paul's last words. Ask the 5 W's and an H to find out what Paul says next.

2 Timothy 4:9 WHAT is Paul's instruction?

"Make every _____ to _____ to me

_____."

Did you put a green box around this instruction?

2 Timothy 4:10 WHAT did we learn about Demas?

Demas _____ this present _____.

He _____ Paul and went to Thessalonica.

2 Timothy 4:11 WHAT do we see about Luke?

Luke is _____ _____.

2 Timothy 4:11 WHY does Paul want Timothy to pick up Mark?

"For he is _____ to me for _____."

2 Timothy 4:13 WHAT does Paul want Timothy to bring?

The _____ and the _____, especially the

_____.

2 Timothy 4:14 WHAT do we see about Alexander the coppersmith?

He did Paul much _____.

WHAT will the Lord do?

The Lord will _____ him according to his

_____.

2 Timothy 4:15 WHAT did Paul tell Timothy to do?

_____ on _____ against him.

WHY? Because he vigorously _____ Paul's

_____.

2 Timothy 4:16 WHAT happened at Paul's first defense?

No one _____ Paul but _____

_____ him.

2 Timothy 4:17 WHO stood with Paul?

The _____

2 Timothy 4:17 WHAT did the Lord do?

He _____ Paul.

WHY? So that the _____ might be

fully _____ and that all the Gentiles

might _____.

Wow! God gave Paul strength so that all the Gentiles could hear the gospel!

2 Timothy 4:17 WHAT do we see about Paul?

He was _____ out of the _____

_____.

2 Timothy 4:18 WHAT will the Lord do?

He will _____ Paul from every _____

_____ and will _____ him _____

to His _____ _____.

2 Timothy 4:21 WHAT is Paul's instruction?

Make every _____ to _____ before

_____.

Does this sound like the same instruction in 4:9?

_____

Did you put a green box around it?

Turn to page 160 and look at 2 Timothy 1:4. WHAT is

Paul longing for? To _____ Timothy.

Paul says this three times. He really wants to see his beloved
son in the faith before he dies.

2 Timothy 4:22 WHAT does Paul ask for? HOW does he
close his letter?

The Lord be with your _____. _____
be with you.

Wow! What an awesome letter! Paul is suffering in prison for
the gospel. He knows his time is short. He knows he is going to
die soon. Paul wants Timothy to pick up Mark and come see him
before the winter. He is alone; only Luke is with him. All of the
others have deserted him. And Alexander did him harm!

But look at WHO stood with Paul, who rescued him and
strengthened him? WHO was it? _____

God never left Paul. Do you know that Hebrews 13:5 tells us that God will never leave or forsake us? He keeps His Word! God was with Paul, rescuing him from every evil deed. And Paul knows that God will bring him safely home. Heaven is our real home, our forever home. How amazing is that? Look at how much God loves you! We may go through trials and suffering, but we are never alone. God is with us. Our divine Coach will always be with us. He will strengthen us and bring us safely to His kingdom!

Now, go back and find all the words in each blank and circle each one of these words in the word search below. And if a word is used more than once, circle it just one time.

P	K	A	O	L	C	S	D	D	R	B	O	O	K	S
R	E	E	S	I	H	D	E	L	E	E	C	A	R	G
O	T	R	U	O	E	E	E	U	P	S	T	O	B	Y
C	E	E	P	N	A	E	D	F	A	T	O	N	M	X
L	A	S	P	S	R	D	W	E	Y	R	D	P	I	E
A	C	C	O	M	P	L	I	S	H	E	D	E	P	W
M	H	U	R	O	D	L	T	U	S	N	P	C	O	O
A	I	E	T	U	N	A	H	E	G	G	E	I	T	B
T	N	D	E	T	D	L	R	O	W	T	U	V	S	S
I	G	A	D	H	S	T	N	E	M	H	C	R	A	P
O	N	Y	L	N	E	V	A	E	H	E	S	E	F	I
N	I	M	O	D	G	N	I	K	A	N	E	S	E	R
T	R	R	V	S	T	R	O	F	F	E	R	V	L	I
I	B	A	E	Y	R	G	U	A	R	D	I	M	Y	T
J	H	H	D	R	O	L	P	A	U	L	S	N	G	O

Great work! Don't forget to practice your memory verse.

Day Five

Going for Gold!

"Good kick, Matthew," Coach Neighbors called out. "Be ready, team. Here they come. Go for the ball, Wes. Pass it to Morgan. Turn, Morgan, turn! There goes the two-minute warning. Come on, Team USA, you can do it! Don't give up—hang in there!"

Coach Neighbors held his breath as Team Brazil headed toward the goal. Josh ran in and intercepted the ball. "All right! All right! Go, Molly! Pass it to Max. Take it, Max. Way to change direction. Great pass. Shoot, Morgan, shoot. You did it! Oh, man—you did it! You won the gold!"

Incredible! Why don't we shoot for gold as we finish up our training in 2 Timothy. Ask God to help you live out your life so that others see Jesus in you!

We're ready to finish our last day. Let's read 2 Timothy 4 and look for the characteristics of a believer—a faithful follower of Christ—and the characteristics of an unbeliever.

Turn to page 164 and read 2 Timothy 4. Look at each verse and fill in the characteristics of a believer in the chart below.

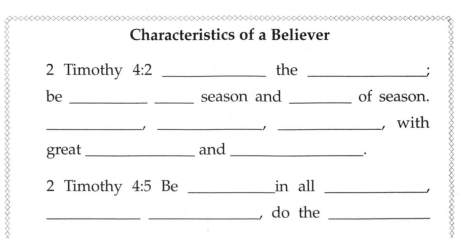

Characteristics of a Believer

2 Timothy 4:2 _____ the _____; be _____ _____ season and _____ of season. _____, _____, _____, with great _____ and _____.

2 Timothy 4:5 Be _____ in all _____, _____ _____, do the _____

of an _____, _____ your

_____.

2 Timothy 4:7 Fight the _____ _____,

_____ the _____, keep the

_____.

2 Timothy 4:8 Will receive the _____ of

_____, loves Jesus'

_____.

Now, read through the verses again. Look for the characteristics of an unbeliever and fill in the chart below.

Characteristics of an Unbeliever

2 Timothy 4:3 They will not _____

_____ _____. They will want to

have their _____ tickled. They will accumu-

late _____ in accordance to their own

_____.

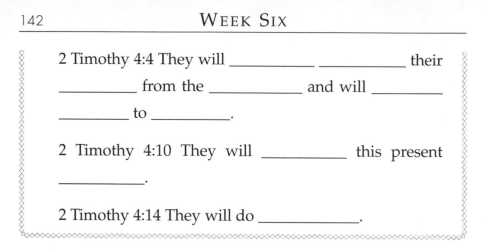

2 Timothy 4:4 They will _____ _____ their

_____ from the _____ and will _____

_____ to _____.

2 Timothy 4:10 They will _____ this present

_____.

2 Timothy 4:14 They will do _____.

All right! You have completed your charts, studied the whole book of 2 Timothy, and seen the characteristics of a true believer (a vessel of honor) and the characteristics of an unbeliever (a vessel of dishonor). Now ask yourself, *WHERE do I fit? Do my actions show that I am a believer? Can others tell by looking at my life that I am different, that I love Jesus?*

Think about what your actions show others. If you need to work on something or change something, go to God and ask Him to help you! Incredible! Find a grown-up, say that last memory verse, and determine to live it out in your life!

Now walk up to the platform. Stand tall and get ready to receive your gold medal. What an amazing performance! You are a true champion for God!

The Closing Ceremony

All right! You did it! You have trained hard, you have finished the course, and you have kept the faith to become a true champion for God! As we participate in the closing ceremony of our summer games, think about all you have learned.

You know that Paul is about to die. He is in prison, suffering for the gospel. But instead of feeling sorry for himself or worrying about his circumstances, Paul writes a letter to Timothy to encourage, instruct, warn, and charge Timothy.

Paul reminds Timothy to stir up the gift that God has given him, to fulfill the call that God has on his life. How about you? Do you know that God has a call on your life too?

You saw Paul tell Timothy not to be ashamed of the gospel, to join him in suffering for the gospel, to retain the standard of sound words, to guard the treasure, and to entrust the gospel to faithful men. *Wow!*

And what did you discover the gospel is? You saw it is revealed through Jesus Christ, and believing the gospel is the only way you can have eternal life. Have you accepted Jesus' awesome gift? Are you ready to share it with others?

You also discovered that you are to be a vessel of honor, careful about whom you hang out with, separating yourself from vessels of dishonor. You are to flee wrong things and pursue righteousness, faith, love, and peace. You are to be careful how you handle God's Word, and you saw that God's Word will equip you to do His work! *Amazing!* We are so proud of you!

Remember, we are living in the last days. Avoid ungodly men, continue in the things you have learned, and be ready to preach the Word at all times!

Here come Max, Molly, and Sam. Max has the baton. Are you ready? Start running, put your hand back… here it comes. Whack! Right into the palm of your hand. Now, hold it tight. Retain it. Guard it. Keep your head down and *run*! You can do it! Don't give up! Pass it on! You are a champion! You can win the gold for God!

Molly, Max, and

(Sam)

P.S. Don't forget to go to www.precept.org/D4Ycertificate to print your special certificate for finishing the course and keeping the faith! We hope you'll join us for another adventure in God's Word real soon!

P.S.S. Max and Molly have a game you might want to play called Believers or Unbelievers.

Just for Fun

You can play Max and Molly's game, Believers or Unbelievers, by yourself or with a friend or family member.

You'll need the game board on page 145, Believers and Unbelievers cards on page 147 and 148 (you'll need to cut those out), a coin to flip, and a marker for each player.

How to play: Place the Believers and Unbelievers cards facedown in the square provided on the game board. Start with your marker on the Start circle. Flip a coin. Heads you move two spaces. Tails you move one space. If you land on a space marked BUB (Believers or Unbelievers), pick up the top card from the pile and follow the instructions. Then return the card to the bottom of the pile. Have fun!

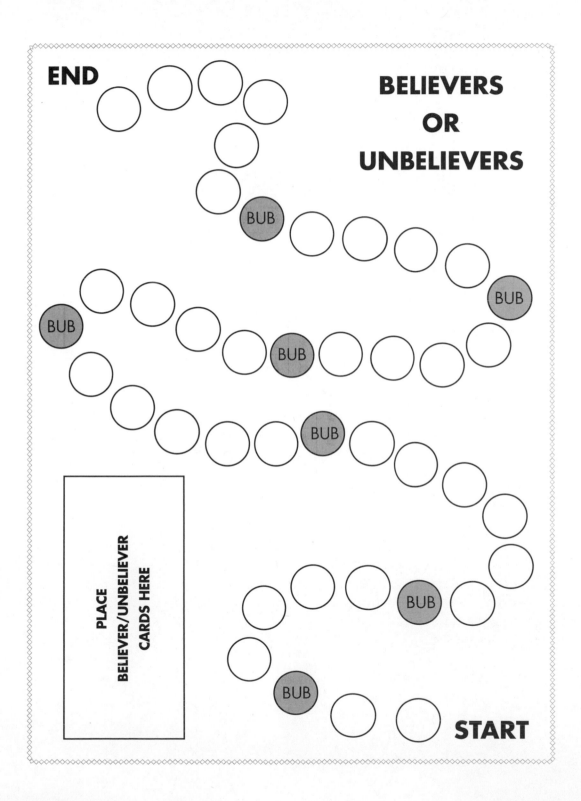

RECITE 2 TIMOTHY 3:14

If you can,
move ahead 3 spaces.

SUFFER FOR GOSPEL

Kids made fun of me for sharing
Jesus. Move ahead 4 spaces.

LOVER OF SELF

Ate the last ice cream instead
of sharing. Go back 2 spaces.

LOVER OF MONEY

Was jealous over my friend's
new iPod. Go back 3 spaces.

INVITED A FRIEND TO
DO A BIBLE STUDY

Move ahead 3 spaces.

I AM GRATEFUL

Told my parents thank you.
Move ahead 2 spaces.

DISOBEDIENT TO PARENTS

Lose a turn.

BOASTFUL

I bragged on my accomplishment.
Go back 2 spaces.

NOT ENTANGLED
WITH WORLD

Told my friends NO to a bad movie.
Move ahead 2 spaces.

PURSUE RIGHTEOUSNESS

Read my Bible every day.
Move ahead 3 spaces.

MALICIOUS GOSSIP

Talked about someone at school.
Lose a turn.

RECITE 2 TIMOTHY 1:14

If you can,
move ahead 2 spaces.

BELIEVER
OR
UNBELIEVER

BELIEVER
OR
UNBELIEVER

BELIEVER
OR
UNBELIEVER

BELIEVER
OR
UNBELIEVER

BELIEVER
OR
UNBELIEVER

BELIEVER
OR
UNBELIEVER

BELIEVER
OR
UNBELIEVER

BELIEVER
OR
UNBELIEVER

BELIEVER
OR
UNBELIEVER

BELIEVER
OR
UNBELIEVER

BELIEVER
OR
UNBELIEVER

BELIEVER
OR
UNBELIEVER

RECITE 2 TIMOTHY 2:15 If you can, move ahead 3 spaces.	**VESSEL OF HONOR** I choose good kids to hang out with. Move ahead 1 space.
CONCEITED I know it all. Go back 1 space.	**A REVILER** I talked bad about a kid to my friend. Go back 2 spaces.
I BELIEVE WHAT THE BIBLE SAYS, NOT WHAT MAN SAYS Move ahead 2 spaces.	**PURSUED LOVE** I prayed for my enemy. Move ahead 3 spaces.
I AM QUARRELSOME I argued with my brother or sister. Lose a turn.	**I USE BAD WORDS** Go back 3 spaces.
CROWN OF RIGHTEOUSNESS I love Jesus' appearing. Move ahead 5 spaces.	**RECITE 2 TIMOTHY 4:5** If you can, move ahead 2 spaces.
I WAS UNLOVING I left someone out. Go back 2 spaces.	**WITHOUT SELF-CONTROL** I lost my temper and slammed the door. Go back 2 spaces.

BELIEVER	BELIEVER
OR	OR
UNBELIEVER	UNBELIEVER

BELIEVER	BELIEVER
OR	OR
UNBELIEVER	UNBELIEVER

BELIEVER	BELIEVER
OR	OR
UNBELIEVER	UNBELIEVER

BELIEVER	BELIEVER
OR	OR
UNBELIEVER	UNBELIEVER

BELIEVER	BELIEVER
OR	OR
UNBELIEVER	UNBELIEVER

BELIEVER	BELIEVER
OR	OR
UNBELIEVER	UNBELIEVER

PUZZLE ANSWERS

Page 13

Guard, through the *Holy Spirit* who *dwells* in *us*, the *treasure* which has been *entrusted* to *you*. 2 Timothy 1:*14*

Page 36

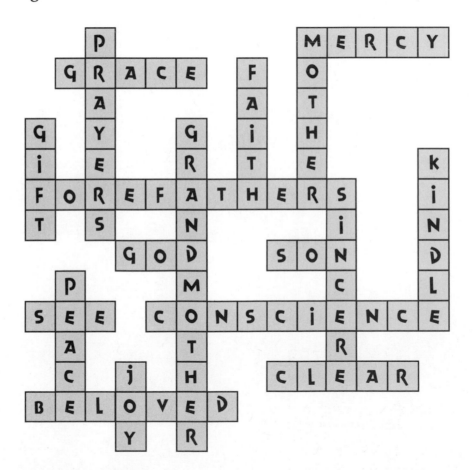

Page 40

who has saved us and called us with a holy calling, not according to our works, but according to His own purpose and grace which was granted us in Christ Jesus from all eternity. 2 Timothy 1:<u>9</u>

Page 61

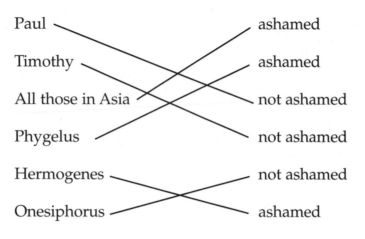

Page 66

Be	swim	diligent	flip	to
Freestyle	present	yourself	stroke	approved
pull	kick	to	God	glide
as	a	butterfly	workman	water
who	does	backstroke	not	need
to	dolphin kick	be	backstroke	ashamed
accurately	racing	handling	the	spin turn
Word	breathe	of	breaststroke	truth.

Be diligent to present yourself approved to God as a workman who does not need to be ashamed, accurately handling the word of truth.

2 Timothy 2:*15*

Page 74

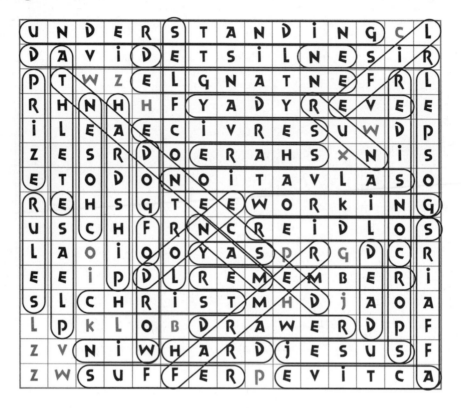

Page 82

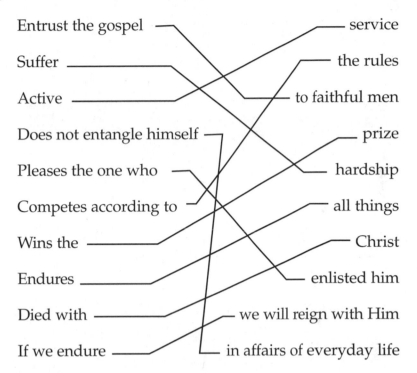

Entrust the gospel — to faithful men

Suffer — hardship

Active — in service

Does not entangle himself — in affairs of everyday life

Pleases the one who — enlisted him

Competes according to — the rules

Wins the — prize

Endures — all things

Died with — we will reign with Him

If we endure — Christ

Pages 84

Now flee from youthful lusts and pursue righteousness, faith, love and peace, with those who call on the Lord from a pure heart.

2 Timothy 2:<u>22</u>

Page 91

Page 107

You, however, _continue_ in the _things_ you have _learned_ and become _convinced_ of, knowing from _whom_ you have _learned_ _them_.

2 Timothy 3:_14_

Page 114

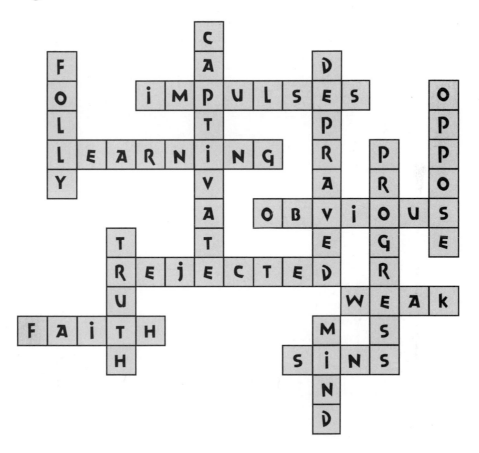

Page 125

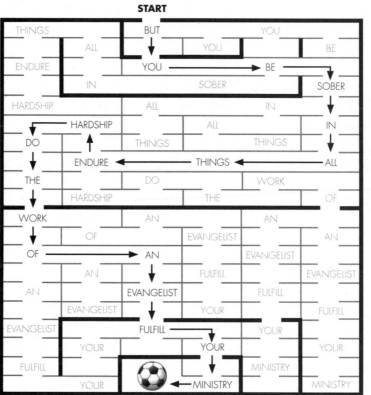

But you, be sober in all things, endure hardship, do the work of an evangelist, fulfill your ministry. 2 Timothy 4:5

Page 139

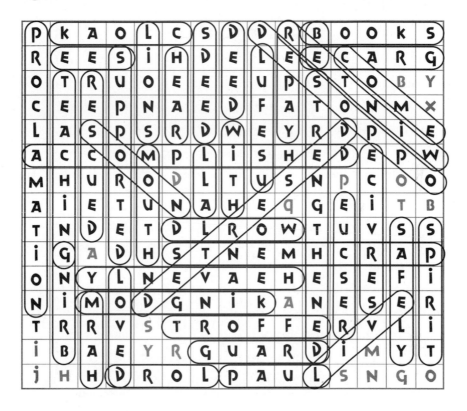

OBSERVATION WORKSHEETS
2 TİMOTHY

Chapter 1

1 Paul, an apostle of Christ Jesus by the will of God, according to the promise of life in Christ Jesus,

2 To Timothy, my beloved son: Grace, mercy and peace from God the Father and Christ Jesus our Lord.

3 I thank God, whom I serve with a clear conscience the way my forefathers did, as I constantly remember you in my prayers night and day,

4 longing to see you, even as I recall your tears, so that I may be filled with joy.

5 For I am mindful of the sincere faith within you, which first dwelt in your grandmother Lois and your mother Eunice, and I am sure that it is in you as well.

6 For this reason I remind you to kindle afresh the gift of God which is in you through the laying on of my hands.

7 For God has not given us a spirit of timidity, but of power and love and discipline.

8 Therefore do not be ashamed of the testimony of our Lord or of me His prisoner, but join with me in suffering for the gospel according to the power of God,

9 who has saved us and called us with a holy calling, not according to our works, but according to His own purpose and grace which was granted us in Christ Jesus from all eternity,

10 but now has been revealed by the appearing of our Savior Christ Jesus, who abolished death and brought life and immortality to light through the gospel,

11 for which I was appointed a preacher and an apostle and a teacher.

12 For this reason I also suffer these things, but I am not ashamed; for I know whom I have believed and I am convinced that He is able to guard what I have entrusted to Him until that day.

13 Retain the standard of sound words which you have heard from me, in the faith and love which are in Christ Jesus.

14 Guard, through the Holy Spirit who dwells in us, the treasure which has been entrusted to you.

15 You are aware of the fact that all who are in Asia turned away from me, among whom are Phygelus and Hermogenes.

16 The Lord grant mercy to the house of Onesiphorus, for he often refreshed me and was not ashamed of my chains;

17 but when he was in Rome, he eagerly searched for me and found me—

18 the Lord grant to him to find mercy from the Lord on that day—and you know very well what services he rendered at Ephesus.

Chapter 2

1 You therefore, my son, be strong in the grace that is in Christ Jesus.

2 The things which you have heard from me in the presence of many witnesses, entrust these to faithful men who will be able to teach others also.

3 Suffer hardship with me, as a good soldier of Christ Jesus.

4 No soldier in active service entangles himself in the affairs of everyday life, so that he may please the one who enlisted him as a soldier.

5 Also if anyone competes as an athlete, he does not win the prize unless he competes according to the rules.

6 The hard-working farmer ought to be the first to receive his share of the crops.

7 Consider what I say, for the Lord will give you understanding in everything.

8 Remember Jesus Christ, risen from the dead, descendant of David, according to my gospel,

9 for which I suffer hardship even to imprisonment as a criminal; but the word of God is not imprisoned.

10 For this reason I endure all things for the sake of those who are chosen, so that they also may obtain the salvation which is in Christ Jesus and with it eternal glory.

11 It is a trustworthy statement:
For if we died with Him, we will also live with Him;

12 If we endure, we will also reign with Him;
If we deny Him, He also will deny us;

13 If we are faithless, He remains faithful, for He cannot deny Himself.

14 Remind them of these things, and solemnly charge them in the presence of God not to wrangle about words, which is useless and leads to the ruin of the hearers.

15 Be diligent to present yourself approved to God as a workman who does not need to be ashamed, accurately handling the word of truth.

16 But avoid worldly and empty chatter, for it will lead to further ungodliness,

17 and their talk will spread like gangrene. Among them are Hymenaeus and Philetus,

18 men who have gone astray from the truth saying that the resurrection has already taken place, and they upset the faith of some.

19 Nevertheless, the firm foundation of God stands, having this seal, "The Lord knows those who are His," and, "Everyone who names the name of the Lord is to abstain from wickedness."

20 Now in a large house there are not only gold and silver vessels,

but also vessels of wood and of earthenware, and some to honor and some to dishonor.

21 Therefore, if anyone cleanses himself from these things, he will be a vessel for honor, sanctified, useful to the Master, prepared for every good work.

22 Now flee from youthful lusts and pursue righteousness, faith, love and peace, with those who call on the Lord from a pure heart.

23 But refuse foolish and ignorant speculations, knowing that they produce quarrels.

24 The Lord's bond-servant must not be quarrelsome, but be kind to all, able to teach, patient when wronged,

25 with gentleness correcting those who are in opposition, if perhaps God may grant them repentance leading to the knowledge of the truth,

26 and they may come to their senses and escape from the snare of the devil, having been held captive by him to do his will.

Chapter 3

1 But realize this, that in the last days difficult times will come.

2 For men will be lovers of self, lovers of money, boastful, arrogant, revilers, disobedient to parents, ungrateful, unholy,

3 unloving, irreconcilable, malicious gossips, without self-control, brutal, haters of good,

4 treacherous, reckless, conceited, lovers of pleasure rather than lovers of God,

5 holding to a form of godliness, although they have denied its power; avoid such men as these.

6 For among them are those who enter into households and captivate weak women weighed down with sins, led on by various impulses,

7 always learning and never able to come to the knowledge of the truth.

8 Just as Jannes and Jambres opposed Moses, so these men also oppose the truth, men of depraved mind, rejected in regard to the faith.

9 But they will not make further progress; for their folly will be obvious to all, just as Jannes's and Jambres's folly was also.

10 Now you followed my teaching, conduct, purpose, faith, patience, love, perseverance,

11 persecutions, and sufferings, such as happened to me at Antioch, at Iconium and at Lystra; what persecutions I endured, and out of them all the Lord rescued me!

12 Indeed, all who desire to live godly in Christ Jesus will be persecuted.

13 But evil men and impostors will proceed from bad to worse, deceiving and being deceived.

14 You, however, continue in the things you have learned and become convinced of, knowing from whom you have learned them,

15 and that from childhood you have known the sacred writings which are able to give you the wisdom that leads to salvation through faith which is in Christ Jesus.

16 All Scripture is inspired by God and profitable for teaching, for reproof, for correction, for training in righteousness;

17 so that the man of God may be adequate, equipped for every good work.

Chapter 4

1 I solemnly charge you in the presence of God and of Christ Jesus, who is to judge the living and the dead, and by His appearing and His kingdom:

2 preach the word; be ready in season and out of season; reprove, rebuke, exhort, with great patience and instruction.

3 For the time will come when they will not endure sound doctrine; but wanting to have their ears tickled, they will accumulate for themselves teachers in accordance to their own desires,

4 and will turn away their ears from the truth and will turn aside to myths.

5 But you, be sober in all things, endure hardship, do the work of an evangelist, fulfill your ministry.

6 For I am already being poured out as a drink offering, and the time of my departure has come.

7 I have fought the good fight, I have finished the course, I have kept the faith;

8 in the future there is laid up for me the crown of righteousness, which the Lord, the righteous Judge, will award to me on that day; and not only to me, but also to all who have loved His appearing.

9 Make every effort to come to me soon;

10 for Demas, having loved this present world, has deserted me and gone to Thessalonica; Crescens has gone to Galatia, Titus to Dalmatia.

11 Only Luke is with me. Pick up Mark and bring him with you, for he is useful to me for service.

12 But Tychicus I have sent to Ephesus.

13 When you come bring the cloak which I left at Troas with Carpus, and the books, especially the parchments.

14 Alexander the coppersmith did me much harm; the Lord will repay him according to his deeds.

15 Be on guard against him yourself, for he vigorously opposed our teaching.

16 At my first defense no one supported me, but all deserted me; may it not be counted against them.

17 But the Lord stood with me and strengthened me, so that through me the proclamation might be fully accomplished, and that all the Gentiles might hear; and I was rescued out of the lion's mouth.

18 The Lord will rescue me from every evil deed, and will bring me safely to His heavenly kingdom; to Him be the glory forever and ever. Amen.

19 Greet Prisca and Aquila, and the household of Onesiphorus.

20 Erastus remained at Corinth, but Trophimus I left sick at Miletus.

21 Make every effort to come before winter. Eubulus greets you, also Pudens and Linus and Claudia and all the brethren.

22 The Lord be with your spirit. Grace be with you.

BRING THE WHOLE COUNSEL OF GOD'S WORD TO KIDS!

▼ **GENESIS**
God's Amazing Creation (Genesis 1–2)
Digging Up the Past (Genesis 3–11)
Abraham, God's Brave Explorer (Genesis 11–25)
Extreme Adventures with God (Genesis 24–36)
Joseph, God's Superhero (Genesis 37–50)

◀ **2 TIMOTHY**
Becoming God's Champion

◀ **JAMES**
Boy, Have I Got Problems!

ESTHER ▶
God Has Big Plans for You, Esther

◀ **REVELATION**
Bible Prophecy for Kids
(Revelation 1–7)
A Sneak Peek into the Future
(Revelation 8–22)

DANIEL ▶
You're a Brave Man, Daniel!
(Daniel 1–6)
Fast-Forward to the Future
(Daniel 7–12)

▲ **TOPICAL & SKILLS**
God, What's Your Name? (Names of God)
Lord, Teach Me to Pray (for Kids)
How to Study Your Bible (for Kids)
also available in DVD
Cracking the Covenant Code (for Kids)

JONAH ▶
Wrong Way, Jonah!

◀ **GOSPEL OF JOHN**
Jesus in the Spotlight (John 1–10)
Jesus—Awesome Power, Awesome Love (John 11–16)
Jesus—To Eternity and Beyond (John 17–21)